WHEN TIME ISN'T ENOUGH

WHEN TIME ISN'T ENOUGH

The Life of Terry Shaffer Hall

Michael Hall

XULON PRESS

Xulon Press
2301 Lucien Way #415
Maitland, FL 32751
407.339.4217
www.xulonpress.com

Unless otherwise indicated, Scripture quotations taken from the New King James Version (NKJV). Copyright © 1982 by Thomas Nelson, Inc. Used by permission. All rights reserved.

Printed in the United States of America.

ISBN-13: 978-1-6305-0759-6

When Time Isn't Enough

Who Will Pick Up the Mantle

WHEN TIME ISN'T ENOUGH

INTRODUCTION

THIS IS BARELY A SMALL BOOK; IT IS more like a long letter dealing with the pain of losing someone close to you—a person you love deeply and with whom you have shared your life. This book is about realizing that no matter how long you had with the one you loved, no amount of time with them is enough when you lose them.

I was blessed to live with the most amazing woman. I share these memories about our inseparable life together, from being young and madly in love to our older years still in love, still loving every day of life together. Our journey of almost forty-nine years ended with her battle with an aggressive cancer that took her life, leaving me devastated over my loss and looking for the strength to comfort a grieving family and a grieving church as a pastor. Inside these few pages, I provide a window into my journey of grief.

You will see that our faith weaves in an out of everything we experienced together. We always welcomed into our life a large circle of different friends—people of our faith, people of other faiths, and people with no religious leanings. We felt our faith was robust enough to exist and grow in the marketplace. I hope you read this even if you aren't a particularly religious person. I'm not a writer by profession, so I apologize that everything I share bounces around quite a bit.

It is my hope that something in these pages helps others who are struggling with the pain of their own loss. This is just a recounting of one husband's grief of losing his wife, yet it is also about how my deep abiding faith has kept me through this. There are no doctrinal arguments here. Is this a religious book? Yes, in part, but please don't let that stop you from reading it.

I'm not trying to change what you believe. In times of crisis, I certainly don't know everything, even in my later years. I just know that you can face this kind of grief at any stage of life. As an old man, who doesn't feel old and is surprised that he is old, I'm still trying to figure things out. Maybe that's why I love being around young people. They give me such hope and have comforted me, even though they are just beginning their journey. I know that my deep, abiding faith in God is helping me through this, sustaining me on my journey that now feels alone without my wife.

You may already be thinking that I should be happy with the forty-nine years of marital bliss. I am, but that is still not enough time to be with the one you love.

As I write this, I know beyond any doubt that I have a heavenly Father who loves you as much as He loves me and He wants to help you through your grief. Just let Him.

OUR LOVE, ROMANCE, AND LIFE TOGETHER

Genesis 2:24 – "Therefore a man shall leave his father and mother and be joined to his wife, and they shall become one flesh."

Proverbs 18:22 – "He who finds a wife finds a good thing, And obtains favor from the Lord."

Colossians 3:14 – "But above all these things put on love, which is the bond of perfection."

Ephesians 5:25 – "Husbands, love your wives, just as Christ also loved the church and gave Himself for her."

OUR ROMANCE, LIFE, AND LOVE together began on June 15, 1970, when my eyes first saw this beautiful young college student selling women's shoes in the store across from the men's clothing store I was managing. She was the most beautiful creature I had ever laid eyes on. She was too young for me, and I was too old for her, but I was smitten. I proceeded to find a way to meet her. Eventually, I did, and we slowly started dating.

Very soon, since neither of us were Christians, we had a little secular wedding ceremony to please me. She said, "Whatever." It would be nine years later when my beloved father would perform a biblical wedding ceremony for us.

I've said before that our relationship started with that first kiss, when I fell madly and forever in love with her. I never got tired of kissing her. We had no idea that this relationship would last within twenty days of forty-nine years. If you are reading this, you are probably a lot younger than me, and in this day of short relationships, I know that over forty-eight years may seem like a lifetime. In my grief, I would like to observe that in this age, there is a noticeable lack of loyalty, and this loyalty is considered old-fashioned, but consider what it has to offer.

What I'm talking about is not some simple, shallow "blind loyalty," but rather an "eyes wide open" commitment to someone you love that takes any kind of separation off the table.

In our search to satisfy what each of us wants, what seems to happen today is we trade in or dispose of anything that doesn't suit us, whether a business, a product, a church, or a mate. The big 'I' reigns supreme over any 'we,' so you probably can't conceive of any kind of relationship that could possibly make you want to spend that much time with one person. But if your relationship is a lifetime of love, passion, adventure, and excitement every single day, from youth into old age, and you are alive and in love each day together, it's because you have invested in that relationship. If you are completely loyal and faithful to your mate, the dividends of that love are incalculable. And each year, it will get better.

My wife and I were so happy that we could live together so long, and we relished each minute of our relationship, which enabled us to easily work together in ministry. Because we loved each other so deeply, it was easy for us to love others. And when we became people of faith, our love became even deeper and more meaningful. Then we understood why we had been put on this earth. We had found a purpose.

In 1982, we bought an old house in Del Ray Alexandria, Virginia. The cheapest in the neighborhood. A wreck. Just the kind Terry loved. Everything needed fixing, from the basement to the attic. The house was one of a kind because, although it was on a busy street, it sat at the back of the lot. She saw no problems with any of it. Her eyes shined when she looked at the house, and with a big smile, she said, "Let's get to work. This is going to be fun!" I should have known, because in every place she rented, we would fix everything, and the owners would shake our hands and say, "Thank you."

Terry remodeled and restored the house. She put a second story on it, had many dump trucks of soil brought in for a beautiful yard, and even built a one-of-a-kind fence around it. We didn't stay in the house because Terry was off to other projects on old houses. And besides, we were not in the remodeling business. It is still one of the prettiest houses for blocks around. Today, it is priced at twenty times what we paid for it, but we don't regret selling it years ago because of all the adventures we've had since. And there was house after house after that.

That's the kind of vision Terry had in everything—most importantly, in people. She could work easily with difficult people, for she saw them and all of us as projects that could be fixed up into something special, and she was so full of love while she was doing it.

I guess my point is maybe that's why Terry loved sharing her faith in Christ and sharing the love of Christ to people who were struggling. She could always see such potential, especially among young women. They would need just a little work — well, maybe a lot of work — but their potential was endless.

When she became a follower of Christ, Terry took His teachings on love seriously. A historian observing the early church stated, "How they love each other" — something I wish more people did today. Terry loved, and she made an effort to live out daily the following verses:

> *Proverbs 10:12 – "Hatred stirs up strife,*
> *But love covers all sins."*

> *1 Peter 4:8 – "And above all things have*
> *fervent love for one another, for 'love*
> *will cover a multitude of sins.'"*

Our Coming to Faith in God

Romans 3:23 – "for all have sinned and fall short of the glory of God…"

Romans 10:9-10 – "if you confess with your mouth the Lord Jesus and believe in your heart that God has raised Him from the dead, you will be saved. [10] For with the heart one believes unto righteousness, and with the mouth confession is made unto salvation."

Romans 1:16 – "For I am not ashamed of the Gospel of Christ, for it is the power of God unto salvation for everyone who believes…"

FOR THE FIRST FEW YEARS OF OUR relationship, I was not a Christian—a person of faith. Even though I had been raised in a Godly home by wonderful parents who were pastors and church planters, I guess I had never really given my life to God. I had never been fully grounded in my parent's firm beliefs. I believed in God, but I wasn't making much of an effort to worship Him. I share this with you because it is my story—it is *our* story—of becoming people of faith.

My life had its ups and downs, mistakes and tragedies, before I met Terry, and yet somehow, God, in His mercy, allowed us to come together and have a wonderful life. Even in this environment, I still never fully surrendered to God. I was thirty-nine when I finally became a Christian.

Now, I am not ashamed to declare my allegiance to Jesus Christ, who is my Lord and Savior. I had dabbled in Native American religions, as well as others, and studied Middle Eastern religions to go along with my interest in martial arts, but they never satisfied me.

One day, my devout mother placed a beautiful Cambridge leather-bound KJV Bible in my hands. She also gave me some C. S. Lewis books. I had never bothered to study historic Christianity before. I had not been impressed with my parents' Pentecostal roots, which seemed overly emotional and not very intellectual, and in my arrogance, I had not taken the time to really study these roots biblically and historically. When I did, I found the Pentecostal faith was a wonderful ancient form of Christian worship. God used these studies to track me down. As I began to read, God's grace soon became irresistible. I realized that He had arrested me and put faith in my heart to believe in Him, and I did. I was a thoroughly converted man.

At that point, I began praying for God to come into Terry's life. She was the love of my life, and I wanted to share with her what I had found, so she could experience what I had. She was the most honest, moral, loving, compassionate person I had ever had any dealings with—much more than many church members I knew. For thirteen years, I prayed every day for God to reveal Himself to Terry.

I tried my best to live a Christian life that would entice Terry to become a person of faith. I witnessed to her in a non-confrontational way because I felt she would never accept a confrontation over what I believed and she didn't.

I answered the call to the ministry and spent the next ten years studying and working in this field. My wife was very proud of me, although I think she thought I was doing some kind of social work, helping people with problems.

But as I grew in the ministry and watched my father's health fail while he battled cancer, a tiny thought that I had rejected for years crossed my mind: *I wonder if he, and the church, might ask me to succeed him.* He had said it to me before, but I didn't take it seriously. With my less-than-perfect past, the prospects of me being a pastor seemed ludicrous. I was happy being a lay minister, and besides, what could I offer? But still I knew that if I were ever called, I could not be a pastor without a wife who was a believer. So, I redoubled my efforts in prayer.

Then one day, after thirteen years of prayer, God tracked her down. We were running from National Airport toward Old Town Alexandria. When you are older, it is hard to believe how fit you were earlier in life. Anyway, Terry must have seen a sad look on my face because she asked why I was upset. I said that I was still praying for her to be saved. That's when she shared the good news that she had come to the Lord. I stopped running and shouted, "Yes!" Yes to my answered prayers. Yes to having my wife work with me in the ministry. Yes to the possibilities of us being a couple of faith. Yes to my life being complete. Terry and the other runners thought I had lost my mind.

We walked the rest of the way home that day, talking about how it had happened, about her spiritual journey.

I almost couldn't believe it. It reminded me of when Peter had been thrown in prison and the early church had prayed and prayed for his release. Well, an angel did just that. Peter walked to the house where everyone was praying for him and knocked on the door. Even when the maid peeked through the door and then told the church Peter was there, the church didn't believe it right away. That was me; I believed it, but I had prayed for so long that at that moment, I almost didn't believe it. But it was real.

There wasn't some huge outward change because Terry was already living a very moral life. In fact, I couldn't see anything that needed changing outwardly. But oh my...the inward change. The love for her Lord that radiated from her was something special. Terry was changed. Her faith in God was so strong, and I knew I had a prayer partner.

Terry immediately immersed herself in reading and studying the Bible, and she soon developed a daily prayer life. I had to move quickly through my studies to keep up with her. She said she had to make up for lost time, which I understood. We both grieved that we hadn't come to Christ earlier in life, but we were grateful for God's grace and the opportunity to serve Him now.

3

A BUSINESS WOMAN

Proverbs 31:10-12 –
"Who can find a virtuous wife?
For her worth is far above rubies.
¹¹ The heart of her husband safely
trusts her;
So he will have no lack of gain.
¹² She does him good and not evil
All the days of her life."

I PAUSE TO INTERJECT THAT FOR A
time, my wife was a successful businesswoman. Terry
had a prosperous career working in the recruiting business. Because of her integrity, she was successful in a
cut-throat work environment. She had grown up in a
business atmosphere with a successful businessman for
a father. She had managed other businesses, so it was
only natural that she would go into business herself.
I have no doubt she would have been extremely successful, but God had other plans.

I was struggling while studying for the ministry, making very little money, but Terry didn't mind, as she made enough for both of us and was preparing to save for our retirement. In fact, one of the reasons Terry went into business was to provide enough income to support me in what I felt was my calling to the ministry. Meanwhile, she was proud that I was doing 'social work.'

Once Terry became a Christian, all I could think about was her working with me. She was in the middle of her career, and no matter how much I wished she could join me in the ministry, I would never have asked her to leave her successful business. At the time, she was recruiting staff for a major political think tank. We had season tickets to the Washington Opera, and we were hanging out with a bunch of friends who were medical professionals—doctors and surgeons. Life was good—in Terry's eyes. But I longed for her to come to work with me in the church.

I guess God understood my prayers. He allowed a recession to wipe out Terry's business, which forced her to sell her building in Old Town Alexandria at an enormous loss. Around the same time, someone stole her favorite car, a little Volkswagen GTI, and destroyed it. Then her father and my father, who had been very ill, both passed away. It was in this climate that I invited her to come to work at the church for fifty dollars per week.

Looking back, I guess God has a way of nudging us in the direction He wants us to go. I am forever grateful that Terry came to work with me. I am also grateful that she had a great hand in developing most of the good qualities I have as a pastor.

What a quiet blessing Terry was to the church and the kingdom of God all these years.

THE HONOR OF SHARING THE GOSPEL AND SHARING THE LOVE OF CHRIST

2 Corinthians 6:3-7 – "We give no offense in anything, that our ministry may not be blamed. ⁴ But in all things we commend ourselves as ministers of God: in much patience, in tribulations, in needs, in distresses, ⁵ in stripes, in imprisonments, in tumults, in labors, in sleeplessness, in fastings; ⁶ by purity, by knowledge, by longsuffering, by kindness, by the Holy Spirit, by sincere love, ⁷ by the word of truth, by the power of God, by the armor of righteousness on the right hand and on the left."

NOW THAT WE WERE WORKING IN THE ministry together, we were barely making enough money to get by. But after looking at St. Paul's description of his ministry, we realized that we weren't suffering at all, so we were thrilled that God had allowed us to be in the ministry.

I was so proud to have Terry with me. As soon as she became a Christian, she immediately started helping me in my work with the church. Even though Terry was a complete novice with everything from Bible Scriptures to hymns to church ways and church lingo, she loved it. She would bemoan the fact that the youngest child knew more about everything in the church than she did. But, she had a sense of humor and a gentle love for God, His Word, new songs, old hymns, and people. Oh, how Terry loved our church, The People's Church.

We do have a most unusual church, full of loving people. Not perfect—none of us are—but what stands out is our love for one another. In our church, we have the honor and pleasure of ministering to people of color. The fact that they accept us with open arms and open hearts is such a powerful witness to the world. We don't have to look just like each other to work together in the kingdom of God, which is exactly what happened in the early church. Over the past few years, God has brought a Hispanic church into our fold. We are all working together, loving each other, and bearing each other's burdens, just like the Bible says.

In the same way that she loved remodeling old houses, Terry jumped right in and went to work with whatever the church needed. And, until shortly before she died, we all acknowledged that she could outwork anyone. She cleaned, painted, picked up supplies; was the church bookkeeper; and went with me to hospitals and homes to visit the sick and shut-ins.

In October 1962, the church first moved into a broken-down old movie theater called the Academy Theater. In the early days, church services had been held there almost every night of the week. Over the years, my father had done his best to repair the building and turn it into a sanctuary, but it soon became rundown again. In 2009, we began remodeling it, and Terry was so excited to work on the building.

The neighborhood was rapidly changing, and a big change was coming for us.

With the demographics quickly shifting, God had other plans for The People's Church. In 2010, He brought Mark and Lora Batterson and NCC into our lives and revealed His plan for NCC to buy our building. Our relationship with Mark and Lora has been the most wonderful blessing to The People's Church.

Because of our close personal and spiritual relationship, we both were able to understand that this was entirely God's doing. Terry and I sold the building to

NCC and moved The People's Church to Maryland, where most of us lived. NCC's ministry on Capitol Hill has exploded, which was God's plan all along. Thank God we got out of the way so that could happen.

When God blessed us to sell the church in DC and move to Camp Springs, Maryland, we saw that this was where He wanted to use us—in a racially mixed neighborhood. We felt right at home. Once we arrived, Terry's business skills were invaluable in helping us acquire, repair, and restore a beautiful old church. She helped with every bit of remodeling, and she was so excited that the teachers and the children had rooms to use for Sunday school and other classes.

Most importantly, Terry poured herself and her love into everyone who came through the doors of the church. She would welcome members with an encouraging hug and invite visitors to be a part of our family. I would hear her say to people, "You have made our church so much better by coming to worship with us."

When God brought Pastor Alveraz, his family, and his Hispanic church to us when they needed a building to worship in, Terry rejoiced because we had so much in this property, and we needed to share it with someone. We thanked God every day for this addition to our family. Each day, Terry was concerned about the immigrant community, no matter where they came from, and she prayed for them and loved them. She faithfully followed God's admonition to Israel about how they should treat the alien, the stranger to their country. Now, you may not agree with her approach, but we will just have to respectfully disagree. I know that Terry's love was real and came from God. As I watched her, I saw Jesus at work through her life, through her words, and through her hands.

Terry's abundance of love extended to our many friends in the Muslim community as well. A young man and dear friend of ours named Driss, who Terry loved like a younger brother, stood at her casket with me and recounted the love he and his family felt for her and their pain of losing her.

Terry loved this country and was so proud and appreciative of those who had fought and laid down their lives for our freedoms. She loved those freedoms, and she prayed daily for our first responders. Of course, while she loved people that looked like her, she also loved and made real friends from Africa, South America, Morocco, Ethiopia, South Africa, Ireland, and Mexico. She stood on *John 3:16: "For God so loved the world..."* She would say, "It says 'world,' not one particular country." Terry counted it a joy to show the love of Christ to everyone she met. She loved the motto of our ministry: "Love God – Love people – Change the world."

She prayed much about the time we are living in—a time of great division. A time of accusations and name calling, when people enjoy demeaning anyone they don't like. A time of threats of violence over petty things, like politics. Terry prayed, as the Bible commands us, for our political leaders. She would pray that God would give them love, compassion, and wisdom. She didn't talk about them; she prayed for them.

Terry had rock-solid personal and biblical beliefs, but she would show love and pray for people on all sides of disagreements. She always kept her politics to herself, unlike me, and voted nationally and locally. When she prayed for this country that she loved, she would pray as our Lord and Savior prayed: "Lord, that we all may be one, Your sight."

I share this with you to show that the love of Christ can step over manmade boundaries. I have never met a person who lived a more righteous and biblically based life of love than my wife. I have never known a more dedicated and devout follower of Jesus Christ than Terry. His love filled her thoughts and her life twenty-four hours a day. She wasn't preachy about her beliefs—she left that to me—but she just loved people with the love of Christ. And I was so proud to be her husband.

She leaves behind an incredible legacy in The People's Church, this wonderful church that she loved and devoted so much of her time to. I believe because of her faithfulness, God has amazing things in store for the church in the future.

GOD'S WORD DID NOT
RETURN VOID

Isaiah 55:11 – "so is My word that
goes out from my mouth:
It will not return to me empty,
but will accomplish what I desire
and achieve the purpose for which
I sent it."

THE CHURCH WASN'T TERRY'S ONLY
focus in the ministry. For twenty-six years, she was
co-director of the US Capital Bible Reading Marathon.

The Bible Reading Marathon is an event that works
alongside the National Day of Prayer, which takes place
the first Thursday in May. On the Sunday night before
the National Day of Prayer, Bible reading begins on the
West Front of the US Capital.

Volunteers would come and stand behind an old
Bible-shaped podium for ninety consecutive hours and

read the entire Bible without comment or commentary. Terry would assemble volunteers from every walk of life — teachers, firemen, policemen, schools, home schoolers, legislators, legislative assistants, pastors, street people, and parishioners.

Reading the Bible in a public place like the US Capitol has been a wonderful celebration of our valued First Amendment rights. Over and over, people from around the world would stand in awe of that liberty.

The Bible reading was not a huge crowd gatherer, but rather a participatory event — and an act of devotion. We didn't raise money, proselytize, or take political or cultural stands. We simply allowed the written Word of God, the Holy Bible, to take precedent through our reading. Terry felt the Bible either has the power to change people or it doesn't. She believed that it did. It had changed her life.

The US Capital Bible Reading Marathon was Terry's heart and soul. She poured every bit of her time and strength into bringing glory to God's written Word. Year by year, as people from around the world walked by while we were reading, she began to assemble 104 non-English translation Bibles for Christian visitors to read, and they did read.

The event was founded by Dr. John Hash and Dr. Corinthia Boone in May of 1990. In 1994, the founders asked us to become co-directors of the Bible reading. For twenty-six years, Terry organized recruited readers, negotiated with venders, and worked with the US Capital Police.

In the last month of her life, Terry attended the handing off of the event to our successors and dear friends, Seedline. Even though she was weak and in pain, she went. Thank God she lived long enough to see her vision continue on. Just another piece of her legacy.

How Will You Fight Your Greatest Battle?

*Romans 8:37 – "in all these things we
are more than conquerors through Him
who loved us."*

*Hebrews 13:5 – "I will never leave you
or forsake you."*

*Psalms 23:4 – "though I walk through
the valley of the shadow of death,
I will fear no evil;
For You are with me;"*

NONE OF US KNOW THE BATTLES WE
will face in life. Terry's greatest and last battle was with
cancer. She was the strongest person I ever knew. Even
when she had to battle cancer, she was strong. In the
beginning of June 2017, Terry was diagnosed with late

stage 3 ovarian cancer, which is frightening enough, but she was also diagnosed with a rare sarcoma, a cancer that is always stage 4 and has no available medical treatment. Soon, Terry had an operation to remove the cancerous tumors and began chemo treatments. Everything looked fine, and we thanked the Lord for bringing her back to health.

However, I was unnerved. Even with my faith in God, I knew this was going to be a battle for both of us. I couldn't believe this woman, who had been so healthy all of her life and was younger than me, was battling a terminal disease. It wasn't right. It wasn't fair. I asked God, "Why don't You take me instead? I'm old. Take me." Now, through tear-filled eyes, I see that He had other plans.

So, I immediately approached the leadership of the church and asked to at least partially retire, so Terry and I could spend time together in Martha's Vineyard, her favorite place. While she was there, she was a different person. No place made her as happy as being on that island. For thirty-three years, we had visited Martha's Vineyard, where we had purchased a tiny apartment and would always relax with a group of wonderful friends.

As Terry struggled to be strong even in her pain, I realized that our long-term plans for traveling up to Martha's Vineyard several times a year were starting to float beyond our grasp. Still, I hoped to somehow have at least five more years with her. I begged God for just five years. Surely, that was possible. I didn't want to think about it, but if God decided to take her, I realized that I would have to come back home to spend my remaining days with my family. Our little island paradise wouldn't be the same without her.

In June 2018, the cancer returned, so Terry had another operation and more chemo. For a while, things were ok. Then her health began to fail once more, little by little. She wouldn't say much, but the pain was becoming constant.

Once a month for seven consecutive months, I had the joy of taking her to Martha's Vineyard, but by early spring of 2019, the cancerous tumors were back with vengeance. The oncology department told us there was nothing more we could do and turned Terry over to hospice.

We kept praying for healing, praying for a remission. People around the country fasted and prayed for Terry. Although she was not afraid of dying, I think she suspected that she might not win this battle, so she began working around the clock, seven days a week, setting her house and the church in order up until the last few days of her life.

As her health began to fail, I asked for and was given the opportunity to be Terry's twenty-four-hour, around-the-clock nurse, along with the hospice nurses. Except for one Sunday morning, when I went to church to preach, I was at her bedside, which was in the living room of our tiny house for ten days. I would pull the sofa next to her bed, and we would hold hands each night as we slept.

We talked, we prayed, and we cried over dreams we would not realize together. In our pain, we leaned on God's comfort through the battle. Each hour of the day, it was a joy for me just to get her anything she wanted, even though that was hard for her, since she had waited on everyone else her whole life.

So many of our children and family came to say goodbye, even though none of us could admit it. Terry would say, "Let's don't talk about me. Tell me about your future. Tell me about your plans. Talk to me about life." I would go to a back bedroom and weep, asking God, "Why?"

I thought back to the last six months, when I sat on the sofa beside her, rubbing her hands and feet for relief from neuropathy, because the chemo had killed the nerves in her feet. Rubbing her lower back to relieve the pressure of the growing tumors. Never realizing how quickly the end was approaching. I did everything

I could to help her without taking away any of her independence. I was with her twenty-four hours a day, trying to keep her alive for as long as possible, but it wasn't enough. There was nothing I could do, nothing anyone could do.

On Thursday and Friday of that week, her health started to fail rapidly, and she was barely conscious and in terrible pain. When she asked me to help stop the pain, it felt like my heart was being torn from my chest.

At 3:00 a.m. Saturday morning, the hospice nurse left our house. Within fifteen minutes, Terry began struggling to breathe. I sat down on the bed and took her into my arms, and for forty-five minutes, with tears streaming down my face, I recounted my love for her and gave thanks for the forty-eight years we had together. I grieved for our dreams that we would not see now.

I wanted to scream, "NO, NO, you can't go! Please keep living. Don't leave me. I can't live without you." But I didn't. In my heart, I just kept pleading, *No this can't be. Not this love, not our life. Our time together can't be ending. Even though it has been almost for-ty-nine years, it is not enough time. Please, God, no!*

These thoughts never became words, because the moment seem too sacred. In my pain and despair at facing the unthinkable, I somehow felt the presence of my heavenly Father giving me strength that I didn't have.

Suddenly, I could feel her slipping away, and there was nothing more I could do. The end came at 4:00 a.m. that Saturday, May 25, 2019, when she died in my arms in our little house by the bay. God took her from my arms and from my breaking heart into, I believe, His arms, close to His heart.

Terry died in the little tear-down house that she had found and completely restored into a beautiful, comfortable, and welcoming retreat by the Chesapeake Bay. Everything on the inside and outside reflected her taste. She had begun having a beautiful fence installed outside of our tiny home just days before she died. Only days after her death, the contractor said to me, "Pastor Mike, she said she was doing this for you," and we all cried.

As devastated as I was at her death, I had a significant funeral to plan. How was I to honor the love of my life of almost forty-nine years? To honor a great woman of God who had impacted so many? To allow people whose lives she had touched share their memories? To do all that in a short time while feeling like a truck had just run over my heart, while stumbling around with tears in my eyes?

The only way I could possibly do it would be with the help of my family and church, so I told my family that I felt we should have the funeral on the following Saturday. Just one week to put together a celebration of her life and death. Only God, my sisters, my niece, my daughter, and my church family made it possible.

Our church was made up of so many families Terry had helped me comfort when they had lost a loved one. Now I was trying to plan the funeral of the one person who was closer to me than anyone on this earth, and I was attempting to do this without her help. Words seemed hollow. Questions seemed strange. The next day, my good friend Ron Taylor II, who was our funeral director, sat in my living room, asking all the questions one must answer for the death certificate. I kept thinking, *We must be talking about someone else, not my darling Terry. She must be alive somewhere. This can't be happening.* Slowly and gently, this young man walked me through the process.

While we were putting together the memorial program with all the pictures, he stopped and asked me to write a letter to Terry for the funeral program.

I moved over to a corner and asked the Lord to help me capture our life in one page. This is my letter to my wife:

My Darling Terry,

You've never been away from me that I didn't know that soon you would be back in my arms and in my life. It has been that way since our first kiss forty-eight years ago. With that one kiss, I fell madly and forever in love with you. What a journey that began. We weren't believers, of course, but down the road we went, we traveled, we rented old broken-down houses that we fixed up. We worked in various interesting jobs just loving life.

I wasn't looking for God, but He saved me nevertheless. I realized that He had chased me down. In fact, now it's clear, He had been stalking both of us for some time. This merciful Heavenly Father, whose grace and love had overwhelmed me, called me to the ministry. I think at first you were amused as I studied for the ministry, but proud that I was doing something nice for people.

I prayed for you. We bought our first house. You bought a building in Old Town Alexandria and opened a business. And I prayed for you. We traveled and enjoyed life because of all that you did. Every minute of every day, I loved being with you. Our life was wonderful. And I prayed for you. For thirteen years, I prayed for you, then God chased you down and saved you.

And God saved you. Did He ever save you. He knew you were supposed to be in the ministry with me, so He took your successful business and income away from you. You said like Job, "The Lord gives and the Lord takes away, blessed is the name of the Lord."

You jumped into the ministry with me, full of love for everyone and a willingness to outwork anyone for the Lord. Eager to pray. God saw your love for His Word and put us in charge of the US Capital Bible Reading Marathon. There you worked helping people from legislators to street people read the Bible in a public place. You singlehandedly assembled 104 non-English Bibles for people to read from other countries, and they came to read.

For twenty-eight years, we have worked side by side building the kingdom of God. Doing whatever He asked. Mostly just sharing Jesus and loving people. As the years passed, we looked forward to the day we could do less work and spend more down time together as we got older. Then two years ago, we found ourselves in a battle with cancer. Being the warrior you were, you fought it week in and week out with all of your strength as we prayed and asked God for deliverance.

That battle ended with you in my arms, Saturday May 25th at 4:00 a.m., when God took you home to heaven.

My arms didn't want to let you go, my heart didn't want to let you go, but I bowed my head and said, "The Lord gives, and the Lord takes away, blessed is the name of the Lord."

I will see you again, my darling. You will be in my arms in a place where there is no night, no sickness, no pain, and no death.

Until then, your loving husband,
Michael

On Friday evening, we had a three-hour wake from 6:00 to 9:00 p.m., where person after person talked about how Terry had impacted their lives. My beloved niece, Cynthia, put together a twenty-two-minute video of pictures, mostly pictures that I had taken of Terry and some of us both, and then set it to beautiful opera music that Terry had loved. People are still watching it and weeping at its beauty.

The funeral was on Saturday at 11:00 a.m. and lasted for over two hours. Other pastors were advising me about what I should do, but I knew that none of them had gone through what I had experienced. So, I said, respectfully, "No, it will be a true memorial because it will all be about her and her life." And it was.

The next day, Sunday, I was able to preach from the topic, "it is well with my soul," the thought taken from an old hymn written by a grieving father who had lost his children. Terry was in the sermon.

Then Monday, I was able to bury her in a short, sweet ceremony with my family and friends. I am so grateful to God that He allowed me four days to honor my sweet Terry.

Terry's Testimony of How She Came to Christ

Mark 16:15 – "And He said to them,
"Go into all the world and preach the
gospel to every creature."

Matthew 5:16 – "Let your light so shine
before men, that they may see your
good works and glorify your Father
in heaven."

Acts 1:8 – "But you shall receive power
when the Holy Spirit has come upon
you; and you shall be witnesses to Me."

Romans 1:16 – "For I am not ashamed
of the gospel of Christ, for it is the
power of God to salvation for everyone
who believes,

ALMOST TWENTY-FIVE YEARS TO THE day Terry died, her beloved nephew found a letter that I believe helped lead him back to God. She wrote him a letter because she loved him and prayed for him daily. In the letter, she shared her concern for him as he was struggling, like we all do at times in our life, in the context of him being the first one in her life to really confront her about her beliefs. It is a powerful defense of the Gospel's transforming grace and power by a woman of deep faith who had struggled to believe in God. This is Terry's nine-page letter to her beloved, amazing nephew Brett, who lives in California. It's long but so powerful:

May 26, 1994

Dear Brett,

   Surprised to receive a letter from your Aunt Terry? I imagine you are. Never wrote to you before; what's the reason to write to you now? Well, for months and months, I have been feeling like I should write to you. Not really feeling like I should, I've been compelled to. Time and time again, the thought comes to mind: Write Brett, and then I think, Why? What do I have to write Brett about all of sudden? I love him, I think about him, get news of him, worry about him, and pray for him all the time—every day, in fact. We all do back here. But he knows that. At least, I hope he knows that.

Anyway, what would Brett think getting a letter from me? Why now, all of a sudden? And what would I say? So, I just ignore the thoughts and go on doing what I'm doing. The problem is that the thoughts won't go away. Right now, I'm in the middle of the very hectic week doing the church newsletter for June. It needs to be done right now, and I'm behind on it and a lot of other pressing things (I've been in Florida with my mom for a week), but the thoughts won't leave me alone this time to do my work. I guess I'll just have to write to you, and maybe then I can finish everything else. I hope my bosses understand; I guess they will. I'm married to one of them.

I've decided to type this because when I started to write first, I couldn't read my own writing! I'm going to warn you, dear Brett, this is probably going to be a long letter. I'm always too long-winded in my writing. That's because I'm basically shy around people, and I never get a chance to talk (especially around Michael and Judy and your Grandmother). So, when I get a chance to address someone, in this case, to write, I must try to get all that suppressed talking out of my system. Please, Brett, read this letter. Don't read it all at once. Who knows how long the letter will take to read? Probably more than any human being would want to read at one time. Read a little at a time, put it aside, read some more later, or maybe the next day. Just read it, Brett. Please.

First things first. We all love you. We're all proud of you. We all think of you every day. I have no idea what you think we think about you. I remember you telling us that your Grandmother had told you that Michael hated you when you were a little kid. That was very wrong. Completely wrong. He loved you then. It was really hard sometimes to love you, because sometimes you were a mean little kid, and you had a smart mouth and you were mean to your mom and beat up your brothers all the time. Other than that, you were great. You were smart and brave and funny and strong and fearless. Most of all, you were our nephew. So, with all the fussing and arguing and throwing your toys on the roof (I know you remember that), we loved you very much when you were a child. No matter what, no matter what you did, we loved you. Still do, though you're a lot nicer and easier to love now.

I bring up the time you were a child because I think about you as a kid a lot these days. For the last few years, I keep remembering something you said to me one day. Again and again, I hear you questioning me. You were a little kid, maybe five or six. One day, you asked me if it was true that I didn't love Jesus. I guess you had just found out that I didn't go to church like all of you and didn't believe in God, or maybe you were just sick of everybody telling you to keep quiet and not harass Terry about not going to church. Whatever, you seemed astonished. How could it be that I didn't love Jesus? Didn't I know that I was going to hell?

Well, I think your whole family held their collective breaths. I was off-limits for witnessing, you see. "Leave her alone," they all said. "She'll find her own way. Just pray for her."

I answered you that no, I didn't believe in God. People felt differently about that, but I knew you did believe in God and your family too, and it was very sweet of you to be concerned about me going to hell. Thanks, but no thanks. You were a very determined little kid, and you knew that Jesus had told us that we were to tell unbelievers about Him and make sure they were saved. So you kept on: "But how can you not believe in Jesus?" It was inconceivable to you then. Eventually, your mom or dad called you off and told you to leave me alone. I was very thankful to be left alone, and I was pretty much left alone until I was thirty-eight. No one else ever witnessed to me as directly as you did.

No one. Can you believe it? In this family of Bible-banging preachers, no one ever again directly confronted me about my salvation as bluntly as you did!

Your Grandmother gave me a Bible with a wonderful, sweet inscription. I never looked at it. They all invited me to church. I didn't go. It made me very uncomfortable to be there. Do you know the feeling? I was very proud of all of them for what they did for a living, but I didn't want any part of church and God. They were unfailingly sweet, and I knew that they loved me and prayed for me all the time. That really bothered me—praying for me. I knew what they were all praying for—my salvation—and that made me uncomfortable. So they did all these sweet, low-key things, but none of them confronted me like you and made me squirm. In the end, none of them ever did. They wanted to, but God knows I wasn't ready to hear it; I wouldn't have accepted it then. When it came twenty years later, it came from a person you won't believe. You really won't believe it. Never, ever could I have imagined who God would use to witness to me in a way I couldn't ignore any longer. But more about that later.

The end of the story is that over three years ago, I accepted Christ. Yes, finally. Can you believe it? Never thought it would happen to Terry? Neither did I! Even more incredible than me becoming a Christian is that my dad had gotten saved earlier that year. Now that is a miracle! Brett, you knew my dad. He was the last person you would ever believe could be saved. He drank—in fact, he was an alcoholic. In spite of that, he was very functional and successful in the business world. He made a lot of money. A lot. Spent a lot and saved for his retirement years. A whole lot. So he was a businessman and very successful, but to his family, he was really cruel, unreasonable, and very verbally abusive.

He was a wonderful monetary provider for us, but he made my mom's life hell for thirty-eight years. I'm surprised she survived it sane. Really. He was immoral: He was never faithful to my mom, and he never was around. Every night, he was in bars until midnight, or usually much later, or out with other women. When he came home, he would be drunk and berate my mom if she didn't have dinner on the table. When he had done something really terrible, we would know because he would come home and pick a huge fight with my mom. Then he would disappear for days, blaming her for picking the fight and doing something he made up.

She never figured out his strategy, and eventually, she would apologize for whatever she could have done and pretty much beg him to forgive her. For what, we never knew. He never apologized to either of us, for anything. When the family was together, it was only at a bar or on a boat trip with his drinking buddies; he would yell and curse at us, tell us we were stupid, and generally humiliate us in front of all of our friends.

On the other hand, he was fun, funny, very generous and loved being around other people.

He loved to kid. You probably remember him like this. He would help anybody, anytime and anywhere.

But every other word out of his mouth was a curse. He truly had the worse mouth of anyone I know, and that includes all the guys here on the street in Southeast Washington. In every sentence, he either said "g d…" or "f…" He never thought anything of it, and if you objected to his language, he told you what you could do.

The point of telling you all of that about my dad was not to tell you what a rotten, mean guy he was. That's no secret, and in the end, it didn't matter how rotten he was. In the end, in spite of all of that, he was saved. Miraculously, mercifully saved by a God who loved him all the time and who forgave him everything. He was saved. And that's the first point of my letter to you.

The second point is that once he was saved, he tried to witness to me, to make sure I was saved before he died.

My father was saved in a hospital room. He wasn't dying then, he was just really sick with a flu, but he did have the terrible lung disease called pulmonary fibrosis. It may have been caused by smoking and drinking or maybe by the chemicals he was exposed to years ago. What the disease did was harden the lining of his lungs so that the air he breathed in couldn't pass through and get into his bloodstream. Slowly, he was going to suffocate to death. There's no treatment, no cure, no hope. But day by day, in his typical way, he didn't believe that. Or at least, we weren't allowed to talk about it, he would cuss us out. He knew he was sick, and he knew the church was praying for him.

He thought they were praying for his health, for healing, but as you probably know, all that time on their knees, they were crying and weeping for his salvation too. If he had known what they were praying for, it would have made him very mad, and he probably would have cussed them out too.

Anyway, he was sick in the hospital, and your Grandpa went to visit him. Somehow, salvation came up in their conversation. Now, you know, that was God, because, like me, no one was allowed to mention anything about that around my dad—ever. He thought it was all 'bulls..." Now, he loved your grandparents and thought they were fine people, doing nice things for "other people." Thought it was nice, but he hated God. He must have, because he cursed God's name every time he opened his mouth.

Anyway, they were talking, John and Fred, not about death, for sure. John was never afraid of anything. He was the toughest man I've ever known. I never heard him admit discomfort, pain, fear, or even the agony he experienced at the end. He suffered a lot, Brett, but I never heard him complain once. Imagine how brave he was, Brett. You and Michael know what it feels like to be choking with asthma, but imagine if there was never any relief for it—no drugs, no oxygen, nothing could help you—ever.

Well, that's how he was living, and he never complained. That's tough and brave and fearless, so I don't think he was telling your grandfather that he was afraid of dying.

But John and Fred were talking, probably like they always talked. Those two were so different but really loved each other. God mercifully made your grandfather half deaf so that he couldn't hear my dad's every other curse word of "g d..." So they were talking that night, maybe about the Redskins, and suddenly, the conversation came around to God and salvation. I'm surprised your grandfather didn't faint or that the angels didn't fall right out of the clouds and heaven. I'll bet they were all hanging pretty far out of the windows of heaven, trying to hear this conversation! I'll bet it got real still and quiet up there. John Shaffer asking about God! Anyway, your grandfather was in shock. He didn't know what to say.

Surely, he had heard my dad wrong…but the Holy Spirit must have made him go ahead. "Well, John,"—can't you just hear him say it, Brett—"are you saying you want to accept Jesus?" My dad said yes, he sure as hell did. Fred explained what real salvation means. No one else ever had. He had never been in a church service. He had never read the Bible. The only time he had ever mentioned God to me was to curse me with His name. So Fred told him that salvation means that you acknowledge Jesus as the Son of God, your Savior, you confess and repent of your sins, and ask Jesus to forgive you and accept you as His own. My dad prayed the sinner's prayer, and that was that.

You can imagine that the telephone lines were sure lit up that night. John got saved! No one believed Fred. Surely, he had misunderstood. So Pastor Robert Green went to the hospital himself.

"Are you a Christian now, John?" "Sure as hell am!" "Well," Bobby said, "let's make sure you really understand what this really means." So Bobby took him through it all, step by step, just to make sure…

Bobby came back. Sure enough, he's saved. "No way! Never!" Michael and I said. He's a thoroughly Godless, mean old man. No way! So Michael went himself. "I heard something from Fred and Bobby, John…" "Yeah! Isn't that great? I became a Christian! D…!" So Michael, like Fred and Bobby, talked to him, questioned him, prayed with him, just to make sure.

Well, garbage, I thought! I had been approaching God myself, tenuously, through the back door, for months. For the first time in my adult life, I was really reaching to God, asking Him to help me believe, but I wasn't ready to take that leap of faith and just believe and say I believed. So I was making my own way, but there was no way that John could have. I simply couldn't buy it. You see, to me, he was still that mean, foulmouthed man he always was.

The guy who was bedridden, crazed on steroids and chemotherapeutic drugs, who cursed and belittled my sweet mom as she waited on him. As she fed, bathed, put him on the potty, wiped him afterward, moved him from bed to wheelchair to the car, lifted him and carried him as fat as he was, he cursed her for not being the one who was going to die. This man accepted Christ and now, therefore, was going to heaven, and my saintly mother was not, simply because she hadn't said those words. No way, simply no way!

I didn't know what it meant, but it couldn't be real. Maybe he was just saved and covering his bases. But no, I should have known that John would never play at salvation. He would never pretend anything. He was just what he was, proud of it, unafraid to tell everyone everything he thought. He was totally blunt and thoughtless of anyone else's feelings. "That's 'bull...' That's stupid...you're an idiot to believe that..." That was my dad's standard way of communicating. So after I thought that through, I realized that he couldn't be pretending, because he was unafraid.

I was uncomfortable with this "new" dad—a "new creation in Christ," supposedly. Brett, believe me, I was watching to see signs of this new man, and he sure didn't seem to be saved or any different to me. You can tell that I sure wasn't saved yet, or I would have realized that it was a change on the inside. He was still the same old mean man, but now he had taken that one and only step that Christ requires for our salvation. He had acknowledged Christ as his Lord.

So Michael and I watched dad. He still cursed, all the time. He was still mean, but not as mean as he had been. He's probably just too sick to fight anymore, I thought. He was still entirely self-absorbed. He didn't care about anyone else. He didn't sleep at night—couldn't—couldn't breathe. So he'd stay up all night and keep the TV blasting. No kidding, like as loud as it would go. That's how he liked it. He would flip channels—cowboy movies and football. Did you know that even in the summer, you can watch football day and night somewhere on cable TV? We needed some rest to be able to take care of him. He was completely helpless and could do nothing for himself. It was a lot of work. But he didn't care. He wouldn't turn the TV down.

We bought him a Bible, a beautiful one in a translation that was easy to read and understand. I'll see if he reads it, I thought. If he's really saved, he'll want to know what God has to say in the Bible. Well, he didn't read it. Never touched it. He just complained about the kind of Bible it was. We didn't understand why he didn't like it, never did understand, and were too hurt to ask.

So his behavior didn't change; he didn't want to know more about God, and he sure couldn't go to the church. Michael would come home from church every day, try to tell him about the sermons, and he just wouldn't say anything. At night, sometimes Michael would go to him alone and ask him if he would listen while Michael read some scriptures and prayed with him. He would get quiet, maybe listening, maybe not, and let Michael do what he wanted to do. But he never talked about his salvation to us.

Anyway, lots went on. It was a pretty terrible way to die, especially for someone so active, so used to doing what he wanted. To be bedridden, helpless, and dependent is an awful fate for someone like him. I remember hearing him gasping for breath at night and cursing, still using God's name, as he tried to take another breath.

In reaction to my dad's supposed salvation, I distanced myself from God. I didn't seek Him so much. I just couldn't accept the idea that is was that easy or that someone as mean as my dad could all of a sudden say those few magic words and, poof, a lifetime of sin and cruelty could disappear. I couldn't buy it. I started running from God again.

One night, we came home to find my dad watching a Billy Graham crusade. Now, that was unique! It was awkward for me. It seemed so ludicrous, so ridiculous, such a farce. My dad, now supposedly saved. I wanted to go downstairs and leave Michael to watch it with him, but he told me to stay. What happened next only took about a minute, but I believe it's what God waited twenty years to say to me. In His incredible, incomprehensible, and awesome way, God used a man as flawed as my dad, toward whom I had lots of hard feelings, to say it to me. Think about it, Brett! This was the second person—you were the first—who really pressed me to choose Christ.

My father had never talked to me about his feelings or anything deep, spiritual, or moral. Never. He couldn't bring himself to ever openly complement me or ever apologize to me, but now he found himself compelled to witness to me. I have to chuckle because now I know what that feels like. Maybe he felt like he should talk to me before, but boy, was it awkward. How to start? He knew what he had put my mom and I through. He knew that ever since I was a little girl, I said I would never get married because of how men treated their wives and how unhappy all the married people I knew were. He knew all that. Now, how could he witness to me?

Well, he did. In his own profane and uncomfortable way with words, he witnessed to his daughter. He tried to make sure that I understood that his decision was for real, and he tried to sell me on salvation for myself in the way he thought would appeal to me, intellectually, with logic. He thought, I guess, that if he could show me the logical reason to accept Christ, I would. I remember he turned down the volume on the TV and said, "Well, look at all those d… Christians there (on TV). That sure as hell is something, isn't it? And I'm one of them! D… right. You know, there are…hell, how many Christians do you think there are? A lot, d…. right! And so how do you think they could all be wrong?"

My dying father's testimony to his daughter. What he was saying was, "I'm saved, and I'm afraid you're not, and I'm afraid for you. Please accept Christ."

I couldn't hear it then, but I've never stopped hearing since. I wasn't ready then. All I heard was a sinner telling me that I should be saved. A lot of nerve. But it made me uncomfortable, like knowing that all those people were praying for me. I couldn't accept it that day, but I did soon after. I did, and I made the confession and the vow that you make when you become a Christian. My dad was still alive, but I never talked to him about it. That's sad, isn't it? But it was typical of our relationship. We never talked about anything, especially anything important.

I am now a Christian. I don't always feel like one. I sure don't always act like one, and I know that a lot of people doubt that I am saved, like I doubted my dad's salvation. But I know that I am. Why? Because I have truly accepted

Christ, and I will tell anyone that He is my Lord. I am compelled to witness. I don't want to all the time. Look, I've refused to write this letter to you for months, though the Holy Spirit clearly told me to do it long ago. And I'm doing it in absolutely the wrong way. I've just written nine pages to a young man who really doesn't like to read. I've had the audacity to witness to a nephew who probably thinks I've never taken a moment to pay attention to him. To some people, I lived an immoral life, living with his uncle nine years before marrying him, and now, all of a sudden, my husband's a pastor and I'm a great spiritual wonder, telling everyone else they should get saved. Pretty obnoxious.

That's how it feels on this end. I really hate writing this. I hate it being so long and so preachy. But, unfortunately, it's not up to me. I believe now, and God commanded me to share His message. He won't leave me alone like I want Him to, to learn and grow quietly in the background. He keeps forcing me into uncomfortable situations, making me do things I don't want to do.

Brett, salvation is the easiest and hardest thing I've ever done. Hard because it was so easy. So hard to say, "I believe in You, Lord," when I really didn't believe it. That's what they call faith. Hard to believe when I'm in a church like this and everyone is going nuts, dancing and speaking in tongues, filled with the Holy Spirit. Everyone but me. It's hard to have faith when everyone around you thinks that if you're not filled with the Holy Spirit, something must be wrong with you or your faith. I've also had friends distance themselves because they're afraid of all the terrible things that have happened to me since I was supposedly saved.

Before I was saved, I had a business, owned a beautiful commercial building in the historic district in Old Town Alexandria. I wouldn't probably get rich on the business, but the building would someday provide the retirement that Michael's profession never would. I was respected in my field as one of the few really honest and honorable recruiters. My clients recommended me to their colleagues for my integrity. Through the business, I was able to talk with fascinating, extraordinarily intelligent, and important people. It was very interesting and always challenging. I was in a wonderful business where I could help people. I could listen to their problems, give them lots of compassion and encouragement, and then help them find a job.

I had a dad who seemed to have a newfound respect for his daughter the businesswoman and a wonderful father-in-law who was sick but hanging on. Family relations were the best they had ever been. I was helping my husband rebuild a relationship with his son, something that had always seemed impossible. I was within a few months of paying off my first mortgage on my home. It had just been appraised for over $200,000, and we would soon owe only $11,000 on it. All that—just think, only ten years before, we had returned from California penniless. I mean, we really had only $1.13 to our name when we rolled back into DC. From nothing to all of that. What a blessed woman I was!

Well, then I was saved. Let's see what happened next. The recession finally killed off my industry, and my business. Suddenly, I was making no money. None. My beautiful building was costing me over $2,000 a month, and I began borrowing money to make the payments. I tried to sell it—for what I paid for it, for less, I didn't care. Just somebody, please, buy it. No one wanted it. Eight months. I was saved, praying every day, lots every day: "Please, God, deliver me from this building. Send someone to buy it. I want to work for Michael in the church. Please." Eight months, not a soul wanted it. $2,000 further in debt every month. My beloved little car, my old, black GTI was stolen and trashed. Two weeks later, my dad died. Horribly.

My sweet, loving father-in-law continued to suffer just as horribly and died soon after. I worked my business every day, hard, really trying. I never made another penny. We were making plans to fly my husband's son here to talk things through and hopefully reconcile some very old and deep problems that kept them apart. He went skiing, had a terrible accident, and became totally paralyzed. His injuries were so horrible that at the time, we didn't think he would live.

A buyer finally appeared for my building, and I praised God. I still thank Him for it, but my friends saw this as a final curse. Selling the building for the price offered put me $45,000 in debt. It will take me twelve years, $500 per month, to pay it off. My house has recently been reappraised: It's worth $149,000 now.

Fell $50,000 in value. We don't know why. So I guess, in the world's terms, my net worth is down $100,000 since I got saved, and I still don't have a penny in the bank. Just a load of credit and bills. So that's how my life has changed since I've gotten saved. Or at least that's how it looks to outsiders. Like it's gone down the tubes. Just like my dad's life looked to me, I'm sure.

No one else can know the depth of love and gratitude I have for the Lord. Like my dad, it's so hard for me to say it out loud. I know I need to speak up in church and give my testimony, but I just can't. Yet. I don't talk like other Christians yet. My vocabulary is still the vocabulary of the world.

I try, but the spiritual words still sound awkward on my lips. I read the Bible every day. Last year, I read the whole thing clear through, and I will again this year. Sometimes it's hard to understand; sometimes I'll read whole chapters and, after I finish, realize that I haven't understood a single thing. We found a wonderful study guide called Bible Pathways that helps. When I read it along with the Bible, I am so blessed. But even with the Bible study, I can't remember things a month or sometimes a week later that were so vivid and profound as I read them. My mind feels like a sieve, and that makes me think about my dad: No wonder he didn't talk about his new faith. He didn't even know the words to use. And the Bible, it must have seemed like a book written in a foreign language without anyone to help lead him and explain things to him. It wouldn't have mattered how easy a translation it was. He must have felt like the only one who didn't understand. Well, sometimes I know how he felt.

When I pray, I always begin by thanking God for all His blessings. I know that I am a very blessed woman. I thank Him for His incredible mercy on me—for accepting me and loving me before, when I didn't love Him, and now, when I sometimes doubt Him. Then I cry. Every time. Without fail. Cry for my unbelief and my former life, but mostly for my father. Two people recently told me that they didn't believe in deathbed salvation. One was a tremendous man of God whose wisdom and power and anointing I'll never approach. The other was a young girl, an unbeliever who reminded me uncannily of myself at a younger age when

I thought I was very deep, knew most everything there is to know, and had worked out all the questions of eternity and God.

Both said they didn't buy it. No way could you live like the devil your whole life and then slide in just before you thought you were going to die. Though I know that I am a novice, a baby Christian, I know they are wrong. I offer my father as the dispute. Even though they, like I used to, probably would doubt the validity of his salvation, I know that he was, and I thank God for it every day. That's the key, the root of it all for me. My God is a God so wonderful, so forgiving, so loving beyond our capacity to understand that He can forgive us anything. He's ready anytime we will finally lay down our stubbornness and accept Him. He's always watching, seeing every horrible thing we do and even think. He knows everything about us, and He still loves us, and He's eternally waiting for us to love Him. That's what makes me weep every time I pray. The thought of His mercy on my father, and then the thought of my dad trying to witness to me.

I pray that I'm through for now with bad things happening. But if I'm not, so be it. I'll still love the Lord. I pray He gives me strength and the faith to keep believing and keep serving Him and keep witnessing. My dad was dying; he was unused to talking about God and could barely gasp for breath, yet he witnessed to me. Long ago, God gave me a gift to write. If I can't yet verbally witness to my loved ones and friends, those whose salvation I pray and weep over daily, like you, Brett, I can at least use the gift He gave me to write my testimony.

I love you. We all do. I'm thinking that if you have actually read this all the way through, you'll probably never speak to me again. I pray the Holy Spirit will go with this letter that I so badly wanted not to write and will open your heart to its message. I've done this in the same spirit that a little boy did for me twenty-some years ago and a dying man did so recently.

God bless you, Brett,
Terry

This powerful recount of Terry's conversion, her testimony, resonates even today. My nephew, as a child, and my father-in-law, John, shortly before he died, witnessing to her were powerful tools in her coming to the

Lord. Her faith was so solidly built on the Scriptures that nothing could ever shake her—not even when she was facing death.

I was also thinking that John didn't live long enough to go to church and learn much about this Christian walk, but he is still witnessing through this letter. With his daughter, he will have won souls to Christ through the letter his daughter wrote, found twenty-five years to the day after she died. I thank God for His grace and goodness.

GOD, ARE YOU STILL THERE?

Ephesians 6:10 – "Finally, my brethren, be strong in the Lord and in the power of His might."

WHEN MY WIFE, TERRY, DIED, I STRUGgled with my broken heart, and I realized that God, with His strength, was going to have to come alongside me in order for me to make it. Overwhelmed with sorrow, I looked at her phone one day and decided to start texting her. I do it on an almost-daily basis. I don't know why I started it, but I soon found that texting her helps me. It's like writing notes to her.

I hope that sharing my pain offers you some hope. I don't want you to think I have given up on life, because I haven't. I'm still pastoring and helping people as an older person. Every day, I'm living out my wife's legacy. The tears still come because my time with her wasn't enough, but I'm going on.

I share these texts as I wrote them on my phone. They are just my raw feelings of grief, not particularly well thought out, but they are what I was feeling at the time. They don't have to be read in any particular order. I don't know, I guess I felt that a couple of months of my texts to her might help you. I wrote them because it helped me, and I hope it helps you. And I believe she is reading them.

Wednesday, May 29th, 7:24 a.m.

My darling, my heart is completely broken. Three days without you. How will I make it?

I'm home darling. Where are you?

I wish you could see the beautiful fence you designed and had built for me. Wait till you see the sign I'm going to put on the side :)

Wednesday, June 5th, 9:45 a.m.

My sweetheart. It's Wednesday, and I woke up with a broken heart. Wanted to fix you a cup of tea this morning. Our daughter, Sheri, is here, and that's good. Keeps me distracted from thinking about my loss. The one-half heart I have left still aches for you.

Thursday, June 6th, 7:18 a.m.

Thursday, my darling. Tough time this morning. Just glanced at a picture, and my heart fell. My beautiful Terry, how I miss your voice.

Friday, June 7th, 12:01 p.m.

Oh my. First trip to our restaurant Hummingbird without you. It's not the same :(

Friday, 7:26 p.m.

My baby. The most amazing woman I ever met. Hope I don't die of a broken heart. I want to spend the rest of my days in the ministry. But how to do it without…

Friday, 11:00 p.m.

Giving some of your clothes to our daughter Sheri as you wished. I probably would have made blankets out of all of your dresses just to be covered with something that was next to your skin.

Sheri looks so pretty in your clothes, so I'll let them go. Just another way you will live on in people's lives. I miss you terribly.

Saturday, June 8th, 7:31 a.m.

My first birthday without you in over 48 years. Since God in His wisdom took you home, I will live for others in your honor.

Saturday, 2:47 p.m.

Well, I made it over to Justin and Cynthia's for my early birthday dinner. Why aren't you with me? My heart is absolutely broken. I just knew you would be there. I miss touching your hand, hearing your voice. Oh, how I miss your voice.

Sunday, June 9th, 10:47 a.m.

My 3rd Sunday without you. Missed praying with you before we left home that God would protect us and that He would allow us to be a blessing to someone.

Monday, June 10th, 7:54 a.m.

Good morning my darling. A quiet rainy morning and all I can think about is how much we loved rainy days. They were cuddle-up days. Fed the cat, getting ready to do my little exercises, but first I have to sit on the side of the bed and cry a little because I miss you so badly today :(

Yesterday at church, it was wonderful to be with everyone and to preach and minister. Pete and Bebe were there from Dallas. But you weren't, and that is my point. I looked for you in so many of the places in the service. I know you are in heaven, and everyone keeps telling me you wouldn't come back if you could, but I would give everything in the world, including my own life, if I could have one more day with you.

Monday, 8:12 p.m.

Why am I wanting to talk to you so much on Monday? I know, Mondays are supposed to be a Pastor's Saturday, a day of R&R. We would sometimes go to your favorite restaurant. Took Sheri to the Mexican place for lunch. Judy joined us for dinner at the Italian place. Walking home, I couldn't stop thinking about holding hands with you. Why are you not here?

People keep trying to help me—so sweet, but it just doesn't work.

Tuesday, June 11th, 7:42 a.m.

Today, Sheri goes home with some of your clothes. I know you are smiling. All those shopping trips make our daughter so happy.

I guess everyone will think my mourning days are officially over. But how can I ever stop grieving when I'm without you, my beautiful, brilliant, loving wife? For 48 years you were the light of my life, and now you are gone. I miss you every minute of the day.

Tuesday, 9:39 p.m.

Why does a perfect marriage make so many people uncomfortable and want to pick it apart? We never ever set our marriage up as an example.

But it doesn't matter, does it? What we had was so wonderful and enjoyable every single day of our life together. Early on, we settled into this loving, respectful, easygoing but madly-in-love partnership that got better every day. That's why people could see the depth of our love just watching us look at each other. And I'm reminded of it every time I look at a picture of you, my darling.

Wednesday, June 12th, 8:29 a.m.

Ok, my darling. I started my early walk. I know you would be happy. You were always so gentle about my weight. What a gracious lady you were. But you're not here to take care of me, so I better work on my fitness. You provided everything else. After all, our bodies are a temple of the Holy Spirit. While I'm grieving you're not here walking with me, you are with me because all I can do is think about you.

Wednesday, 10:13 p.m.

Goodnight, my darling. Just me and the cat on the bed. How comforting it was to be able to just reach over and touch you through the night to make sure you were there. I would always smile in the dark and drift back to sleep. Safe and sound with my sweetheart. Knowing we would always smile at each other when we woke up. Wonderful memories.

Thursday, June 13th, 7:12 a.m.

A windy, rainy, stormy morning on the bay. The shallow waters kicking up small waves like their big brother in the ocean. We would both sit on the sofa with our bare feet touching on the coffee table. You with your hot tea, holding the cup with both of your beautiful hands. Just content sitting together, not saying anything, enjoying God's creation and each other.

I always loved and admired your quiet, strong faith in God. It's not that you didn't worry about things; you did. You needed to balance out my carefree nature. You were the one who always planned for our future. You were the one who always worked out a plan to get to our goals. Each day was a step toward those goals. That systematic way of living kept us on track. And that is the way you lived out your faith.

Thursday, 9:41 a.m.

It's been 20 days since I've held your beautiful face and kissed those precious lips. 20 long days since you took my face in your hands and kissed me and smiled that smile that made everything in my life light up.

It's amazing—as much as we both loved music and even those English mysteries you loved, we were completely comfortable with silence. In MV, when we would hike long trails that led to the sea, we would sit on a rock, looking at the water, holding hands. We would sit for the longest time without saying anything, and it was ok because my heart was talking to your heart.

Thursday, 10:20 p.m.

Not quite three weeks since you've been gone. I can see in people's eyes who aren't that close to me that I need to be thinking about all the big things to do in the ministry. They don't know that the pain is as raw as the day you left. They don't know that I will never be alright without you.

I will never be whole again. They don't know that I just want to stay in this house close to your things, close to your dreams, close to where you were.

Friday, June 14th, 7:13 a.m.

The sun is shining today, but it's cloudy and raining in my heart. I forgot to tell you after your wake how many people shared that you made a powerful impact on their lives. And at your incredible funeral, you were so honored. You would have been so uncomfortable because it was all about you and your amazing life. Tracy said about your funeral that she had never seen over 200 people weep for two hours. Well, we all did because we lost you. We wept and still do because of the chunk of our lives that is now missing.

Friday, 5:31 p.m.

Well, it's June 14, and Judy and I took Irene out for a late birthday lunch. Wanted to show her some comfort and love. Went back to her house and just listened to her talk about you. Of course, I could listen to anyone talk about you for hours. And you know I could talk about you for hours. From the day I met you, you have endlessly fascinated me. I wonder what Adam and Eve talked about.

Saturday, June 15th, 7:08 a.m.

Good morning, my sweet wife. I had a dream that this was all a frightening nightmare that I was trying to wake up from. That you would be here. That you would be healthy again and in no pain. That everything would be like it once was before the great battle that you fought so bravely. That I hadn't lost you to that battle. That I would wake up and reach over and touch you like I did every day for almost 49 years. That later in the day, we would be carefree, smiling, laughing. In the middle of one of your fascination projects. But I woke up alone with just my memories of you.

Saturday, 8:23 a.m.

Three weeks to the day that I lost you. People use words like "passed way," "transitioned," "graduated," "homegoing," "gone to a better place," I guess to soften the blow. But really, it doesn't make someone's death any easier to the loved one left behind.

And we tend to say to our friends, "I know what you are going through," when we don't until we experience it. Nevertheless, I appreciate their attempts to comfort me. And I'm thankful for their love and comfort.

A slow, sunny Saturday morning. The day before the Lord's day, when we would be preparing for worship on Sunday. You would each Saturday prayerfully select the "call to worship" scriptures, and they would always be the right ones. And we would try to wrap up the projects of the week.

No matter what we had to do or where we had to go, you would deftly balance, organize, and pull it together, and I would go to sleep knowing that Sunday coming on would be wonderful, because of you.

Seems like mornings are so sad now. As I sit and read my Bible through my tears, I think about you, and then I begin to pray. And it seems the Lord wraps me in His arms and says, "My grace is sufficient for you," and the day starts to get better. Then the phone rings, and my dear friend Scott says, "I'm on the other side of the Chesapeake Bay, looking at you." A coincidence? I don't think so.

Saturday, 10:13 a.m.

Why do I talk to you so much on Saturday? I don't know. Maybe because you were so easy to talk to. You had an amazing ability to give me your undivided attention and listen. I learned that from you. We would talk and listen to each other, or sit and just drink each other in with our eyes. Then you would say, "This is the day the Lord has made; let us rejoice and be glad in it." And off we would go on some adventure.

Saturday, 10:22 p.m.

Time for bed Saturday evening. Preparing for my fourth Sunday without you is so lonely. You were such a powerful prayer partner and had such godly wisdom. And God would use you so often to direct me in how I should minister. How do I do that now? I know God is with me, but my helpmate is not with me. I will go on alone. People say to me, "Your smile is coming back." But when they look in my eyes, they see the sadness that will never go away.

Sunday, June 16th, 7:15 a.m.

Good morning, my beautiful Terry. It's my fourth Sunday without you, and it's Father's Day. I have to be encouraging to the fathers. I promised the church that I would not be morose and sad forever, but inside, I think I probably will. But my job is to lift people up and encourage them while I'm teaching them about God. I'm asking God to comfort and lift my spirit. And then I start to remember our amazing, wonderful life, and a tiny bit of a smile starts. I'm the most blessed man in the world because I am Terry's husband. You made me happy and content for over 48 years. I can share some of that. And I can share that God is good.

We used to watch old couples walk slowly together holding hands. We would smile and tell each other that would be us someday. Never once thinking it might not happen. But now when I walk, I reach for your hand, but you're not there. And yet I'm not alone. My Shepherd is with me. His rod and His staff comfort me. He will be with me on the rest of my journey.

Sunday, 2:25 p.m.

Well, made it home after church. It was great preaching about the Holy Spirit. Another of my ministers has decided to leave. But I just love our church so much. Don't know what God is doing, but I know that He does all things well. I always admired you for being happy about whether God was bringing people in or leading people out. You never "numbered Israel."

People keep dropping in, surprised we are going on and doing just fine without them. They don't even know what God is doing and is about to do.

Our kitty misses you. She knows how lonesome I am for my sweetheart. Sometimes she just lays down on the arm of the chair I'm slouched in, as if to say, "Come on, Pops. We can make it." And you know what? I know we can make it, just this little lonesome twosome. Kitty and me.

Sunday 6:45 p.m.

Almost 7 p.m. Most of Sunday is behind me. The fourth Sunday since you've been gone. I'm at a loss as to what I should do with the evening. I haven't been able to turn the TV on. What's there to watch? Don't know how I can watch what we watched together.

Monday, June 17th, 7:36 a.m.

Good morning, Terry. Just finished my breakfast. Having a few minutes in prayer before I go on my walk. Will you go with me? Anyway, looking at our front room in our small house, I realize I haven't put the large coffee table back. I keep saying, "Well, it leaves more room for visitors." But really, I think it's because it is the spot where your hospital bed was. It still feels like a sacred place to me. We spent our last days, hours, and minutes together there. It was there that God lifted you from my arms to His.

Someone said that when God comes for us, our loved ones will be there to greet us. I don't know if that's true, but I hope so. I hope you are there to greet me. To welcome me to the place we both talked about so often. In that place where we will be with the Lord forever and ever. I hope you take me in your arms and then take my hand again. I hope we walk hand and hand again. Then my broken heart will be mended. Then my tears will stop, and my pain will stop, and once again I can laugh with real joy.

Monday, 10:42 a.m.

Apostle Paul speaks of our eternal destiny this way: "To be absent from the body is to be present with the Lord." Paul was a tent maker, and he understood that tents are temporary, just as these bodies are temporary. But God has something better for us. A body that will live forever without pain, sickness, aging, or dying.

Terry, you were amazing here. I can't wait to see you in your new body. What does it feel like? I'm sorry, I know you are the most beautiful woman in heaven.

Tuesday, June 18th, 7:19

Tuesday morning. It rained last night. Actually, the storms on the bay with lightning and lots of thunder are impressive. We would sit close together on the sofa and watch the display of God's power in bringing needed rain, and we would be thankful while we're being entertained. Whether we were walking, hiking, biking, or traveling in a car, you always marveled at God's creation.

You made me slow down from whatever I was doing that I thought was important. You would say, "Stop! Look at this." It always made me feel closer to God. Thank you.

It's strange to reach this age. I'm 80, but I don't feel 80. I don't know how old I feel, but certainly not THAT old. I wonder if all older people feel younger. We always did. I still do. I just don't have my young wife with me.

And people have started treating me like some elderly sage who has suddenly acquired great wisdom. I wish you were here. You were always so wise in everything. I'm still trying to figure all of this out.

I miss so many things about you. I miss sitting holding your hand, looking into your beautiful eyes, and talking about our plans; you always made plans. That gave me something to look forward to. Everything we have is because of your plans. I was just along for the ride.

Now, it seems that God has other plans. I'm trying to adjust my life to those plans. It's not easy.

I just realized something, and I don't know if any other husband can say this. In every picture I have of us when you are kissing me, you are smiling that beautiful smile. And as I thought back through those 48-plus years, I remembered that every time you kissed me, you not only gave me a kiss; you gave me a loving smile as you looked at me. Why was I so blessed to have you as my lover, my wife, my adviser, my companion, my prayer partner? Thank you, God, for these precious memories.

Wednesday, June 19th, 8:01 a.m.

Was thinking this morning about young people, people a lot younger than me. About them living in a time where there is so little loyalty to anything. Whether it is a product, a business, a church, or a person. It mostly depends on what they do for us. Drop one and pick up another with hardly a thought. The great "I" must be pleased at all costs. My 48 years with my wife were delightful because it was never about I, it was always about us. And we were committed to being an "us," no matter what. That's why we had so much fun right up to the last week. Every day was an exciting journey. A day to interact with people. To learn. To experience. To help. Every night a comfortable retreat to our home. Day in and day out, we enjoyed each other.

Wednesday, 10:08 p.m.

Goodnight, my darling. In bed thinking of you, missing you. Just the kitty curled up in her little bed and me on my side reaching over to touch you, but you're not there. Empty house without you, but I'm grateful for all you did to make it so beautiful and cozy. Just me and memories of you. What fun we always had together. You laughed at all of my jokes and when I acted crazy. It's funny we never felt old, but of course, you weren't. I was, but you pretended I wasn't, and being married to a younger wife sure made me happy. I wish God had left you here with me. Someday, I'll know why He took you home.

Friday, June 21st, 7:14 a.m.

Good morning, my love. Have to go to two banks today for church business. Trying to help several people get all the business affairs of the church running as smoothly as you did. All of us trying to work together to do what one person did.

No matter whether we were, here or out of town, you were working on something for the church. I don't know if anyone in the church ever knew how many hours a week you devoted to your part of the ministry. I know they loved you and you loved them; that's why you never complained. How pleasing to God and a lesson to all of us. God give us a servant's heart.

Saturday, 10:36 p.m.

Busy day, my darling. How did you do it all? Banks, accountant, at church looking for the bylaws for the bank, and on and on. Every time I get into the car, I think about you. When I'm driving, I turn to ask you something or tell you that you are beautiful, which you always were, and that I love you. I always felt complete when I was with you. I keep thinking how much you wanted to go to Full Kee, our favorite Chinese restaurant, for some won ton soup. I don't know if I can ever go back without you.

My trip to MV with Ralph for only three days is coming up, and I'm going to be a mess. I leaned on you for so many things. What will I do now?

Saturday, June 22nd, 8:58 a.m.

Good morning, my sweet. It's Saturday, Sunday preparation day for pastors. I can't believe I slept in till 8:15.

The cat too. I woke up much earlier than our usual time of getting up. I laid there thinking about you, and then I began dreaming about you. I guess I didn't want the dream to end. But it seemed when I woke up, you were saying to me, in that voice that I never tired of hearing, "Michael, get up. There are things to do today. And you have to go on." So, I got up. I walked through our little house and called your name several times just to hear it myself. The cat looked sad, and I sighed.

Will our pets go to heaven? What a frivolous thought to many, including people of faith. But of course, they are part of God's beautiful creation, and the Bible says that after He had created everything, He looked at it and said that it was good. Why am I thinking about this? Because I find our kitty in your little office looking around for you, meowing quietly. Sleeping on everything and just looking generally confused. She's looking for you. She misses you. C. S. Lewis thought we would see our pets in heaven. I hope so. Then she will understand.

Saturday, 10:57 a.m.

Running into the church to check on some things and pick up the mail. You would always be with me, whether it was a short trip or long. To the store or just getting gas. People would laugh at us because they never saw one without the other. They would say that we were joined at the hip, and we were.

Guys were always trying to find ways of being away from their wives and with their buddies. I was always trying to figure out ways of spending time with you. They would tease me, but really, I had more fun being with you. I guess when God made us one, He really did.

Saturday, 3:18 p.m.

Went for my walk in the late afternoon today, down to the boardwalk in North Beach. All the couples were walking hand in hand. I sat on one of the memorial benches, looking out on the bay. Wish I had a memorial bench for you, but they are all taken here. I have some plans for our little cottage by the bay. I want it to be a surprise to you, because I know you're watching. I'm plugging along as fast as an 80-year-old can, I guess. Everything I do, I think about you. That keeps me going because I see you in everything.

Saturday, 9:41 p.m.

Heading for bed. Have to speak for Mark Batterson tomorrow morning in our old church building. The last Sunday service there. So much history in that building. So wish you could be with me.

Now I can say it. Four weeks to the day since I lost you. This has been a tough day. Lots of tears. Everything is making me cry. I will never get over losing you. What we had was so special and unusual. Our love. I haven't even been able to put your pictures out yet. I can see how people die of a broken heart. Really asking God to comfort me, and I know He will, but I'm hurting right now.

Sunday, June 23rd, 3:37 p.m.

Wow! It's 3:30, and I haven't texted you since yesterday. Been talking to you and about you all day. Preached twice for Mark this morning and headed out to go to the new location at 5:30. They are dedicating it for a grand opening next Sunday. So pleased with what God is doing with NCC.

Just couldn't believe you weren't with me. My life is so hollow without you, and yet I am grateful for the wonderful life we had together. Everyone is expecting you to be with me, and when I tell them why you're not with me, then the tears come. I love you, my darling, for time and eternity.

Sunday, 8:57 p.m.

Ok, home from an amazing dedication of NCC's new place at 8th and M St. The praise and worship team were awesome. Just sat and enjoyed the service and what God is doing through Mark and his team.

Just cried over and over wanting you to be there. You always enjoyed their services—told Mark that. Love our church more than anything, but I guess God is going to make sure the connection stays intact. God must have a reason. I just want to be a blessing wherever I go. It's a little harder without you.

Did I tell you that I'm putting my thoughts together for a little book about you? I know, I know you never want anyone talking about the great things you do, but I'm gonna do it. Might as well get used to it because the Lord is going to help me.

Monday, June 24th, 9:15 a.m.

Sitting at the Toyota dealership while they service the 4Runner, and you're not here for the first time. So many sad firsts that I'll have to go through.

People keep saying it's ok because you are looking down on me. Well, that's fine, but I want you here; I need you here. There is no one on earth who could take your place.

No drama ever. Just a calm and enduring love. I'm reminded of that as I hear people fussing and fighting on their phones. I guess we did have a perfect marriage. We were so blessed.

Weeping may endure for a night, but joy comes in the morning. So the psalmist says. My weeping certainly endures. I guess my joy comes from being a blessing to others and helping whoever I can. I know you would want me to carry on our legacy. A young man asked me last night what I thought the most important thing in the ministry was. I immediately thought of you and said, "Just love people."

Monday, 3:37 p.m.

Oh, my darling. How can life go on without you? Everything around me, everyone around me, seems so normal. Don't they know the huge loss to this world because you're gone? Don't they see the gaping hole in everything because you're not there? Don't they realize that half of my heart is gone? Don't they know this can't be fixed? Don't they know that your laughter still echoes in my heart and your smile is still imprinted in my mind? But I can't touch you, I can't kiss you, I can't hear you. Don't they see how sad I really am? Missing you on a hot, steamy summer day. If you were here, we would go for ice cream.

Monday, 10:26 p.m.

Goodnight, sweet princess. I guess you don't have to sleep in heaven. I can't even imagine how glorious it must be. I'm puttering along in this old body, thinking of you, knowing that just the sight of you would thrill me. Do you know I still love you? We are husband and wife for time and eternity. When I finally get to see you, no matter how many years will have passed here, it will be just a moment in eternity. The best day of my life will be when I see you again, my love.

I know people think I'm selfish for having a life with an extraordinary woman for almost 49 years and wanting more when so many people have so few with their mates. And lonely people who have no one. They are right—I am selfish. Partially, in my defense, I think we both were open to everyone about how special we thought our life was. So yes, I'm selfish for wanting more, but grateful for every day and thankful for pictures and memories. Thank you, dear God.

Tuesday, June 25th, 9:01 a.m.

A late good morning, my darling. I have to catch up on my writing. I just thought I would let you know. You are always in my thoughts and my heart. Just stopped at the closet this morning and held one of your coats.

Just the smallest whiff of your presence in that coat brought a torrent of tears and memories. I hung it up and put it aside, like you did with your beautiful body when you went to be with the Lord.

Tuesday, 9:25 p.m.

Ok, goodnight, sweet forever wife. Spent some time on your book. I'll let it sit awhile so some thoughts can percolate in my brain and memory.

It's been a month, and the pain is just as raw as when I lost you. I'll just have to put my trust in the Lord and pray that He carries me through all of this. So many things I want to talk to you about. Do you see me? Do you hear me?

I'm sad at all the people who will never know you and experience your loving testimony of your faith. What a loss. I guess that's why I'm trying to make you come alive in my little book. You were so special. Did you know that people who never met you weep at just hearing about you? What a legacy!

Wednesday, June 26th, 7:27 a.m.

This morning as I was waking up, I drifted in and out of sleep, in and out of dreams where we would be talking. Conversation then silence, conversation then silence. I got up, fed the cat, got my breakfast of toast and a protein drink. When you were here, I would hear the teapot whistle, the cabinet door open and close, the water turn on and off, the toaster pop up, you pouring your tea, and then the sounds of your bare feet as you came to join me for breakfast. Sounds that I once took for granted replaced by silence. I miss the sound of you.

Wednesday, 9:33 a.m.

I feel pretty good most of the time, but I'm grieving the rest. I just sit quietly, thinking about you, wondering if I can make it without you. No matter how many people need me, I don't know. You fought so hard to live. I would watch you, my darling, pushing yourself to do things. I was in awe of your quiet strength. I don't think I have that. I'm just longing to see you. Wanting to hold you. Desperate to talk to you. The Lord is with me, I know, but this is a valley of sorrow.

The Psalmist said, "Though I walk through the valley of the shadow of death, You are with me." Not that death is always near us, but the shadow of death. Just the shadow of a predator frightened the sheep. The shadow of death that took you doesn't frighten me, but because it became more than a shadow, I grieve. But I must continue on my journey because it leads to you.

Wednesday, 9:43 p.m.

Goodnight, my darling. This day has had its ups and downs. Had fun with Ralph getting toys for us. But this afternoon and evening, I have really been down.

This afternoon, I was so lonely for you that I decided to watch your video but completely lost it about five minutes in. Couldn't stop crying. Was sad all through the service tonight.

Thursday, June 27th, 10:51 a.m.

Good morning. I guess there are no mornings or nights in heaven, but I'm still here...Anyway, my darling, I'm struggling without you, and I guess this is normal. Although, there doesn't seem to be anything normal about this. People keep telling me this is my new normal. I want my old one back.

Thursday, 10:51 a.m.

I am so glad for God's words "I'll never leave you or forsake you." What a comfort that is to me. It's not like any family or friend has forsaken me; they hover around me, concerned. But when you are grieving, even in a crowd, you can feel alone. But knowing He is always there to lead you and guide you, that's something to be grateful for.

Thursday, 8:37 p.m.

Another end of the day without you. The sun is almost down. Watching it slowly get dark. It is so quiet in our little house. I haven't had the TV on since you left. Just don't see how I can watch anything we watched together and pay attention to it. I am so out of everything. Care nothing for any pop culture or sports or drama or much of anything else. Maybe that will change in time. Right now, all I want to do is think about you, remember you, miss you, and long for you. Oh, how I long for you. I hope I will make you proud. I guess you'll tell me when I see you.

Friday, June 28th, 7:40 a.m.

Good morning. Yet another day without you. Till I die, I will not stop counting the days. I know people will get tired of comforting me. And I have to adjust to life without you. But how to do that. I can't forget anything about you. I don't want to forget anything. I'm trying to wrap up writing this little book about you. Put together something for someone to read, to see if I'm on the right track. There is so much about you I want to put in it, if I could just find the right words.

You know, I was thinking, my darling. I've hardly taken any pictures on my phone since you've been gone. I always wanted to document everything we did together, especially around the church. But without you in the picture or standing beside me, I struggle for inspiration. Yes, you certainly inspired me, always. Miss that.

Job said, "Till I die, I will not put away my integrity from me." May I live that every day. You certainly did, in a world that suddenly decided not to.

Friday, 4:59 p.m.

A quiet, hot summer afternoon. What would we be doing? Maybe going for a walk, having some ice cream. You always loved chocolate chip and also chocolate gelato.

So many things that you liked to eat that I just can't yet. Maybe someday. I wonder if the pain will ever lessen so I can talk about you without crying. I know that at some point, people will probably get tired of that. I want to share the joy you brought me every day we were together, my darling Terry.

Friday, 8:05 p.m.

Oh, my sweet. Again, the sun is going down in our little house that you rebuilt, remodeled, and furnished to fit your taste. It's quiet so much of the time now. No TV or music, just the cat talking to the birds and me in my recliner, talking to you in this text. The cat looks at me when I sigh. You would always ask me why am I sighing, and I wouldn't know. Now I do. Just so many beautiful memories drifting through my mind of you. You were so beautiful, from the first day I met you till the day I said goodbye. How could I have been so blessed?

Saturday, June 29th, 8:03 a.m.

Good Saturday morning, love of my life. Well, today I'm going with Ralph to pay for our toys. A toy you didn't want to have while you were here but said I could if you left. Of course, it's a more age-appropriate toy now. I hope you're ok with it. Just wish you were here, because we did everything together.

Saturday, 3:59 p.m.

Thinking about going to our little Italian place just two blocks from here. Got me thinking about the amazing Italian feasts we used to put on. What a cook you were. That marinara sauce bubbling in one of our giant pots. Homemade meat balls roasting in the oven. Mushrooms sautéing in a large skillet in olive oil and garlic. That antipasto salad on one of our huge platters, with salami and pastrami and prosciutto and provolone cheese and olives and much more with great olive oil and red wine vinegar. Fresh basil chopped to be used wherever. Fresh baked crusty Catania Italian bread, with olive oil for dipping and the smell of garlic hovering over everything.

Saturday, 9:54 p.m.

Goodnight, my darling. People can't get me off the subject of you. I love it. And they can't believe how wonderful you really were. How much I loved every idea you had, every place you wanted to go, every project you wanted to get us involved in. They think I disappeared into you. But we really believe that in marriage, God made you and me one. They saw me supporting you and your ideas but failed to see how much time, effort, love, prayers, and support you gave me for my ministry. Just like I think I helped you in everything, I know that you helped me immensely in being a pastor. Thank you, because you're still giving yourself unselfishly to me because of all you did.

Sunday, June 30th, 6:55 a.m.

Well, it's my sixth Sunday without you. I'm trying to get used to the other half of me being gone, and I don't think I ever will. My wonderful "we" has become a diminished "me." But I believe that God can use less to do more. So, in His name and your memory, I am going to accomplish something meaningful for His kingdom.

Someone said that a big part of doing something is just showing up. Well, let's show up today and see what God is going to do.

Oh my, it's Sunday. Tomorrow morning, early, the cat and I will pick up Ralph, and we will head to MV to dismantle our dream. I'm afraid I'll be a mess from beginning to end. So many things we had planned to do and enjoy, even being there part time. Now, I must draw the curtain on 33 years of memories. I don't want to…but without you, the experience would be too painful. I'm so happy we found this place. I'll relive our memories over and over. Of course, in them, we are always young and having so much fun just being there. Thanks for the memories, my darling.

This is the Lord's Day, the day He has made. I will rejoice and be glad in it. I will lift up my praise to Him because He is worthy of all praise. I will worship Him in the beauty of holiness. I will sing and pray and preach His Word and minister to His people. I will thank Him for walking with me through the shadow of the valley of death. He is bringing me through a dark place because He is light and in Him is no darkness at all. Thank you, God, for the time You allowed me to have with Terry.

Sunday, 10:19 a.m.

At church. Such a huge hole in everything without you here. You would be running back and forth from your office to mine, getting everything ready for morning worship. You always had such an uplifting attitude that made every Sunday service full of joy. Even when you were so sick that you had to come downstairs and lay down, you kept pushing the church forward until you were confined to a bed. What a load you gladly carried.

Sunday, 7:37 p.m.

Well, getting stuff together to pick up Ralph at 6:30 a.m.
for 3 days in MV. I guess I'm dismantling our dream.
33 years of dreams brought to a close. Oh, the memo-
ries from the time we would leave for the trip. I wish
I could sit with you for hours just to talk about MV. I
will be going through everything, touching your things,
smelling your clothes, looking at how you decorated the
apartment. My beautiful, talented Terry.

Sunday, 9:33 p.m.

Goodnight, my one and only love. Why did you have
to leave me? I'm the old one. I should have gone first.
Really. I'll never understand God's plans till I get on
the other side. I do have questions, even though I'm
not questioning God. I'm so limited without you. How
can I accomplish a fraction of what we did together?
I understand why people of old went into monasteries
when their spouses died. But I will try in your honor
because you would want me to.

Monday, July 1st, 11:03 a.m.

Well, it's the middle of the day. Headed to MV, Ralph is
driving, just came over the Tappen Zee bridge...trying
to text; it's hard—bumpy road and tear-filled eyes.

Monday, 12:26 p.m.

At Brandfort, CT, for gas and pit stop. How am I doing this without you, my darling? Memory after memory. The tears come and go. So glad Ralph came, or it would be a sad trip for kitty and me.

Monday, 3:33 p.m.

My goodness. We are over 3 hours early. No stand by because it is summer. Never had that experience. Anyway, we'll just wait for the 7:30 boat. Go looking for some food. Wish you were here.

Wandering around Falmouth, killing time and looking for a fast food place. I keep wanting to call you and talk to you.

Monday, 6:37 p.m.

Grief counselor called me, checking on me. Told her I was doing fine. Lots of support. Now all of a sudden, I feel so alone without you. Got on the 6:30 ferry, remembering so many times here with you. It can never be the same. Our dreams are shattered, completely. Could not have made it without Ralph.

Monday, 10:43 p.m.

Well, late to be going to bed. Coming to grips with the fact that without you, our dreams in MV are finished. The memories are endless and all good. But I don't know if, or how many times, I will be back here. People are wonderful and comforting, and I appreciate it. I think God wants me to live out my life and your legacy back home.

Tuesday, July 2nd, 6:38 a.m.

Ok. The day begins. Put together boxes and start packing up our life that was to be here on MV—that's the plan. In every closet, in every drawer, on every wall, looking at every piece of furniture, sitting on the porch looking at the ocean, I think of you. Your handprints are on everything, including my heart. Memories of us doing so many little unimportant things, but now they are important to me. Will they live on in my mind when I leave here?

Whether we went to the grocery store, Reliable market, to the hardware, to the bakery, to Menemsha for lobster, to the Black Dog for cookies, or to visit friends, or for a walk by the water or even to church, we always went together. Everyone always saw us together. We were always together, and now we are not. I'm kind of lost. How do I do anything without the most important person in my life? I will somehow.

Tuesday, 8:09 p.m.

Well, darling, as brokenhearted as I am without you, I'm wanting to hang on to our place in MV. Or at least thinking about it. Not for a long time because I don't think I will be away from you a long time. Maybe a couple years. Enough time for family and friends to come and see what you created for us. Very proud of you, my darling baby.

Tuesday, 9:28 p.m.

I've laughed a few times since you've been gone, but I haven't smiled. Every time I saw you or you looked at me, I smiled. No matter how I was feeling, you could always make me smile. Today, I had a little smile here in MV thinking and talking about you and our times here. Was that from you?

In my sorrow, I still thank God for His goodness, His mercy, His love, and His grace. I know He cares that I'm grieving. You were always so mindful of that when I occasionally forgot to be. You were always such an example to me. I guess I will have to be the example for both of us now.

Wednesday, July 3rd, 7:07 a.m.

"Another day in paradise," we would always say while here on our little island. Now, what do I say? I guess I can say, "Another day in the place of Terry's dreams." I'm starting to see that since you always worked so hard at everything, you relished being in a place of peace and beauty. A place to relax and enjoy God's creation. A place to get away from your nonstop work, even though you always brought it with you. You would say, "The work of the Lord has to go on." And you would smile while working for a while, and then we would go play.

Wednesday, 10:41 a.m.

A wave of sadness washed over me. Just told Mike that you were gone. While I was talking to him, I realized all the work he has done for us, but without you and our dream, I won't need him anymore.

Everything we did here, every person we knew, suddenly, I realize it's in the past and I'm stuck between the past and the present. What is this place that I am in? God took the better half of us. He's going to have quite a job getting me to do a fraction of what you did, but I'll try for you. I want you to be proud of me.

Wednesday, 7:27 p.m.

Well, my darling, Ralph and I have been packing up all of our stuff to take home. Away from our little paradise in MV. Trying to decide what to leave here. So many things remind me of you. Pictures, mirrors, cans of Cento tomatoes, olive oil, the special shower curtain, the most comfortable king-size bed in the world, and the porch furniture. Oh my. I know I have to leave some of you here because it makes this place special, otherwise I would strip it clean.

Thursday, July 4th, 7:31 a.m.

Good morning, beautiful Terry. Another sunny day on MV. Here I am in this very special place you created for us, but without you, something is always lacking. Your presence, your voice, your ideas, your personality, and your smile. I'm crying this morning thinking about that smile. Even to the last, you would smile at me. And then you would kiss me.

Thursday, 12:40 p.m.

Had your favorite breakfast at Linda Jeans with Cynthia and Josh—blueberry pancakes. Took Addie's real maple syrup with us. What fun we would always have, the two of us. You always sat looking outside at the beautiful view, me looking at something far more beautiful—you.

Thursday, 7:17 p.m.

Well, day is almost done. Everything is packed for in the morning. Can't take it all, but we have most of our personal things going home. The dismantling of most of our dream. So much is still here. It will take several trips before I can decide what to take home. It's all you. Everything, you carefully picked out everything here. Every beautiful serving platter or dish that is so perfect here reflects you.

Thursday, 9:08 p.m.

The hydrangeas were all blooming; with the new paint, the house looks so tidy and fresh. You would be so happy and proud. Tom has done a great job. He and Mary and the girls have been so comforting to me.

I keep seeing couples everywhere, and while I'm happy to see them in love, I want to stop them and say, "Make each minute count. You can't get a single one back."

Friday July 5th, 6:33 a.m.

Good morning, love. Think we've got everything packed. Ralph and I did a pretty good job, but you were so organized.

Getting on the ferry at Oak Bluffs. Looking back at our house. First time I've ever left MV without you. I'm so sad. I think Chappy is sad too. What happened to our dream? So much of it packed in the car to take home. Each time I come up, I will have to bring lots of framed pictures of you. I'll be the grieving old man with the forever young and beautiful wife. And that's ok because the rest of my life will be about your memories and your legacy.

Saturday, July 6th, 8:21 a.m.

Good morning, my beautiful Terry. Back in Chesapeake Beach. Yesterday the trip from MV to MD was so hard to make without you. We came the long way, the one you didn't like, so that helped a little. On our regular route, everything reminds me of you. Had a picture of you kissing me on the dash. It was a comfort, but sometimes I cried. Then I would glance through the sunroof up through the blue skies and wonder what you were doing. Well, I've got to get busy unloading our memories from MV this morning. I have to tell you, when I was driving back into our little town, your memories and your presence started to make me feel I can make it.

And when I came into our little house, the house that you made entirely for us, the house with your handprints on everything, I felt at home. I felt the peace of God. That is all because of you, my beautiful baby.

Saturday, 9:36 p.m.

Goodnight, my darling. Tomorrow will be my seventh Sunday without you. I've come to the conclusion it will never get easier, because you meant so much to me. I'm a pastor, so I will go tomorrow and take care of the sheep. Our precious church that we both love so much.

I will never get over losing you. Oh, God, you made us one; why did You take her and leave me here? You must have a reason. I believe my life is part of Your divine plan. Help me to understand it, please.

Sunday, July 7th, 10:58 a.m.

Rev. Stratton told me her daughter Jasmine's dream of you coming into the church for choir practice, beautifully dressed in white. Sitting for a while then leaving, as if you were satisfied that all was well.

Sunday, 9:53 p.m.

Well, it's bedtime in our little house. Just me and the kitty wishing you were here. Actually, we sat in the living room as the sun went down, thinking of you and how much we miss you. Just quietly thinking about another

Sunday without you. Speaking of we, it will always be we—Michael and Terry.

Goodnight, my beautiful wife. I hope I see you in my dreams.

Monday, July 8th, 9:04 a.m.

A late good morning. I love you more than ever. I know people may think I'm a little off for doing this, but I call your name out loud several times a day, just to hear it. The kitty's ears prick up, and she looks around. And I talk to you often. If you are getting tired of me doing all the talking, well, you can speak anytime you want. I would love to hear anything from you.

Monday, July 8th, 9:31 p.m.

Well, my days are busy, and that is good. I see you in everything I do. The pain has lessened a little today. It will never go away, and I realize it so much when I go to sleep alone, knowing I will wake without the love of my life. My darling, no one can ever take your place. Talking to our daughter Rahel about a memorial to you. About creating or coming alongside of something that was important to you. We are going to make sure that you live on and that you are never forgotten. Yes. You are that special, my love.

Tuesday, July 9th, 7:05 a.m.

Good morning. Another bright, sunny, humid summer day. As much as you enjoyed winter and snow, you never complained about the summer heat. Really, you never complained about anything. You just took every-thing in stride. There was simply no bad weather ever, if you were near the water. I guess that's why we have two small places where we can see the water. I love it because it reminds me of you.

"The Lord is my Shepherd, I shall not want." You took that to mean working on a plan to live debt free as much as possible. Old-timers called it cash only. Basing our giving on the OT principle of tithes, the giving of a minimum 10% to God. You always gave more. And then attempting to save 10%. And finally, living within our means. You said that was a biblical principle that would allow us to help others. You were right.

And that is just one aspect of that line from the 23rd Psalm. By doing those things and doing what St. Paul said, being content with what we have, God has sup-plied all of our needs.

And now He is supplying me with comfort and strength, enabling me to go on without you when I didn't think I could. Your presence and memory and legacy are all with me. But of course, that will never be enough, because I want you physically here with me. Nevertheless, my Shepherd is always with me.

Tuesday, 11:52 a.m.

At Costco's, having lunch and picking up stuff. You always asked me why I was in such a hurry when we were here. I don't know. I always was in a hurry. Would give anything to be here with you, taking our time.

Tuesday, 9:59 p.m.

Had a wonderful evening with Ralph and Judy, Jerry and Troyce, and Jeremy Caleb and Gabrielle. Fixed steamed shrimp to go with Ralph's macaroni salad.

Afterward, the girls went through your leather coats and your jewelry. I was hesitant to start giving away your stuff. But Troyce and Gabby were doing it so respectfully, with tears in their eyes; I know you will love seeing it on them. Also separated things for Sheri, Roni, Cynthia, and Brenda. Just another way for you to live on. You will never be forgotten by anyone. It is helping me deal with my grief. I just feel your presence here in our little house by the Bay. Goodnight, my darling.

Wednesday, July 10th, 9:19 a.m.

Well, a late good morning. Finished breakfast, sitting here looking at the Bay and thinking of our walk with the Lord as people of faith. There was always so much spiritual strength in your walk. I treasure that. It made me stronger. I miss you, my darling, but your presence and your prayers live on in me. You were so quiet but powerful as a woman of God. You were one of His special creations, and I can't wait to see you.

Thursday, July 11th, 8:00 a.m.

Good morning, sweetheart. I'm so sorry I only texted you once yesterday. You were on my mind constantly. Went to Hummingbird with the family and saw Val. He said Janice is having a ball in our apt. on MV. He's joining her on Saturday. You always wanted to get them up there for all that Val had done for us through the years.

And Carla, your buddy in the battle, texted me this morning. I'll see her next trip up. Then I'll have a couple extra days to talk to everyone about you. I'm starting to get excited about all the ways you will live on with so many people. I love you, my darling.

Thursday, 9:00 a.m.

Oh, Lord, I miss Terry so much! People around me, close to me, are getting on with life. They hope I'm doing better, and in some small ways, I am, but I'm really not. There are glimpses of humor here and there. And I feel good when I'm doing something for God and His kingdom. Their wounds will heal; mine will not heal, ever. How can they, without Terry?

Just sitting here this morning, all I can think of is how I miss my precious wife. How I miss her love, her presence, her voice, her prayers. It reminds me of an old, old song,
"I'll never smile again, until I smile at you. I'll never laugh again, what good would it do?"

I wonder about people outside this beautiful little white house by the Bay. A house whose remodeling and decorating reflects your taste of living by the water. Which shows in every detail your ability to take something worn out and broken down and make it beautiful. Which is home to the old man you did this for. I wonder if they wonder why I am so sad all the time. I'm sad because you're not here with me, and I'm sad because they will never know the incredible woman you were.

Friday, July 12th, 8:21 p.m.

Wow! A whole day without texting you. Ralph and I were at motorcycle school trying to relearn how to ride. Five and a half hours on hot bikes, 91 degrees all on asphalt. We were thirty years older than the oldest student. It was brutal for old guys like us. Both got home with severely cramping legs. Eating bananas and drinking Gatorade. You would have been chuckling at us. Just trying to get a license, so we can pick up our Trikes on Monday. Love you, my darling.

Saturday, July 12th, 7:22 a.m.

Good morning, my darling. Well, the two old guys are back at the motorcycle school. Another 90-plus day to wear us out. Last day, thank goodness. Wish you were. I would convince you to ride with me on our Trike. You would love it.

Just kind of fell apart coming down here to Hughsville, MD, thinking about you. No matter how many people are around, I'm always lonely for you, my beautiful darling. Why are you not with me? Why have our dreams been shattered? Only God knows.

Saturday, 3:33 p.m.

Well, I'm home. Graduated motorcycle safety riding class that MD mandates now. Ralph and I are completely whipped. What's not hurting is cramping and hurting. Now, we'll have to go through all kinds of DMV stuff for our license. Will get the bikes next week, sometime. It was tough at 80.

Sure missed you cheering me on like you always did with everything I did, and I hope I did for you. What a loving wife you were. I miss you so much.

Saturday, 5:02 p.m.

Late Saturday afternoon. Sitting in my chair, listening to lawnmowers around me. The cat is snoozing. I'm working on my sermon for tomorrow. Looking at the Bay and wishing for you. You would be so busy getting ready for tomorrow. I'm trying, Sweetie, but so many things are being left undone. What a force you were. I miss you so much. I need your advice. It was always just right.

Saturday, 9:14 p.m.

Almost time to go to bed. Still haven't had the TV on since you left. Get my news on my phone. I'll turn it on again someday, but I'll never be able to watch it like we did together for an hour or two at night. Strange, isn't it? So many empty spots in my life now. But God is in my life in a special way, and for that I'm grateful. I'll just let Him use me as He sees fit.

Goodnight, my darling. Tomorrow is my 8th Sunday without you. Are you watching over me? Do you know how much I love you and always will? Do you know that no one would ever take your place? You are my beloved wife for time and eternity. I'll be with you soon. I know you are waiting for me.

Sunday, July 14th, 6:56 a.m.

Good morning, sweetheart. There will never be a morning without you that doesn't sadden me. My 8th Sunday without you. I will eat breakfast alone, get in the car alone, go to church alone, come home alone, and go to bed alone. That's how it feels since you're not here. You filled so much of my life with joy. Your voice, your laugh. I loved everything you did. You were wonderful. My life and this old world is diminished without you.

The question I battle every single day is, how do I go on without you? Without the love of my life. Without the joy and light of my life. Here I am almost two months out from losing you, and several times a day I get sad and weepy. Family and friends are totally back to normal, and I understand that; they want me to go and do things. But I want to spend as much time here in our little house where I last held you in my arms. This is the place where I feel your presence most.

Sunday, 7:30 p.m.

Well, we had a good service today. Brittany sang, "God Is" in praise and worship, not knowing I would be preaching from the 23rd Psalm with the title, "The Lord Is." Amazing how God works so often. Judy wanted Ralph and me to go over to Justin's for BBQ, but we were so whipped, we headed for home. It sure takes a while for old guys to recover.

Talked to your mom a little while ago. She's still grieving, like me. The loss for both of us is incalculable. She's so lonely. Don't you worry, I will never abandon her. We just talk and talk about how amazing you were. About how many lives you touched. You, my angel, were very, very special.

Sunday, 9:42 p.m.

Goodnight, my darling. Without you, I don't seem to fit in anymore. I had heard that about widows and widowers. Now I'm one. I'm not an outsider exactly, not an insider either. Strange feeling. All I can say is the Lord is my Shepherd. And I'm so thrilled—I found the t-shirt you slept in. What a treasure. It smells of you. I'll sleep better. Love you, darling.

Monday, July 15th, 7:31 p.m.

Well, here it is another day; all day and I haven't texted you. Not that I haven't started to a couple of times.

Justin found a seafood and crab place north of Annapolis. It's an hour away, and Judy came down to ride with me. I kind of protested the whole way. But then we got there, the Point Crab and Grill. Right by the river. Completely open to the outside. Boats pulling right up and people getting off and walking in. Food was great. Old time funky place in the middle of a boatyard. Just the kind of place you would love, we would love.

Wish I could go back there tomorrow with you, my love. So many great eating places you searched out for us. Ambience may not have been top notch, but the food was always spectacular. You just had that knack for finding such interesting places that live on in my memory, whether they are still in business or not. How blessed am I that God gave me the most amazing woman and wife who left me with a lifetime of wonderful memories?

Thank you, my love, for making life worth living, even without you here with me.

Monday, 9:15 p.m.

How do I go on without you? My family, who loves you, is trying to help me, and I do fine part of the time. But just driving to Annapolis from our little house is so full of memories of you, I can hardly do it. I don't want to experience anything without you. You were with me in almost everything I did. I guess I'll sleep on it. Trying to figure out what to do. Goodnight, my darling. There will never be a night in my life I don't say that.

Tuesday, July 16th, 6:30 a.m.

Good morning, sweet, beautiful, wonderful, amazing wife. Love of my life. Wife for time and eternity. I love you.

Tuesday, 7:25 p.m.

Well, what a day. It went by in a blur. Met Ralph and Jerry at the HD dealership to look at our Trikes that we will pick up tomorrow.

On the way down, I cried several times thinking about you, about how beautiful you were in so many ways. Thinking about how much I will miss you every single day of my life. I tell God that every day in prayer. I guess I'm just asking for comfort from the pain. He is my only comfort. He knows I'm suffering.

And the Trikes, just something to fill empty hours now and then, because without you, all my hours are empty. I miss you, my darling.

I know why you wanted out of here so badly. It wasn't just your love for MV, even though you always wanted to move there. From the beginning of the cancer diagnosis, you were afraid. It wasn't lack of faith; you had faith. It was a horrendous enemy, this cancer that was attacking you. You wanted to get up there as soon as you could so we could have time together. I was afraid from the beginning as well.

Oh, why did we lose this battle…

Goodnight, my darling. Just looking at some pictures of you. You were beautiful from the day I met you till I lost you.

Our relationship was so very special. You overlooked so many of my shortcomings. I thought about that as I looked at those pictures. What a gracious woman you were, and how God used that part of your personality to bless so many people. How do I become more like you?

Wednesday, July 17th, 7:47 a.m.

Good morning, my darling. I don't want you, and especially God, to think I am wandering around in my misery without being grateful. Yes, I'm struggling without you; I always will. But I'm so grateful to God for almost 49 incredible years with you. And, I'm so grateful for His grace and His mercy for saving you and me. That's why I will carry on His work without you. I will continue your legacy because you loved the Lord so much and you loved people. So how can I not show the love of Christ to everyone I meet? God help me to continue to do that.

Wednesday, 9:06 p.m.

Nearing the end of a hot summer day. The clouds have been black and threatening all afternoon and evening. Lots of powerful thunderstorms. Kind of matches my mood today and this evening. Just so despondent without you. Sometimes I think I could almost die of a broken heart. I know that people do. When you yearn so much for the one that has gone that nothing, absolutely nothing or nobody, can cheer you. Yes, I know that God is here, but I miss my darling.

Rita preached a wonderful midweek sermon tonight about the Holy Spirit helping us pray when sometimes we are so far down all we can do is groan. The Holy Spirit makes those groans and sobs into articulate prayers. That has been what my prayers sounded like today. Groaning and moaning as I called out to God and as I talked to you. My broken heart is hurting so badly. I want to do so many things with you, but you're not here. I don't even want to experience new things without you. How will I share them with you? Back to my inarticulate praying.

Thursday, July 18th, 7:47 a.m.

Good morning, sweetheart. Praying for a better day today. Yesterday was disheartening. I was thankful to be able to go to church and pray and be ministered to.

I needed to pour out my heart to God in a place of prayer. Relief didn't come last night, but I feel a little better today. I must learn to give God time to work.

How can I minister to people with strength? How can I minister help and hope when I'm so broken? Maybe in my brokenness, I'll understand their burdens. I know from God's Word that He understands my loss and suffering. Lord, help me to life up those around me.

Well, the gloom is starting to fade. Going to ride my Trike to the church this morning to check on something that was close to your heart, VBC. Want to encourage Pastor Stratton and all the wonderful helpers who are teaching young ones about the love of Christ. I know you are with me in spirit.

Thursday, 11:50 a.m.

Stopping at Popeyes. What do you want me to pick up for you?

Thursday, 4:45 p.m.

Ok. Late afternoon of a 99-degree summer day. Back at home working on my little book about you. I think I'm going to make it. Today, as I was riding my Trike, not closed in a car, I could look all around at God's beautiful creation. And somehow, I felt you looking down at me and smiling that beautiful smile. I realized that not only is He with me at all times, you are as well. My darling, my darling, watch over me.

Friday, July 19th, 8:05 a.m.

Good morning, my darling. For the first time in almost two months, I feel like my spirits have been lifted. Have you lifted my spirits? Are you telling me I am approaching the end of my official mourning? I will always grieve, every single day, but are you saying I need to get on with the work God has for me to do? Are you telling me to look at God's beautiful creation and enjoy your memories? Sitting here this morning, looking at the Bay in the little house that you built, with tears in my eyes, I'm telling you that I will try. I love you, my darling.

What does life hold for me now, this forever-married man who has lost his beloved wife? I will always be married to you, and I will always be waiting to see you and hold you in my arms again. There will always be an underlying sadness because you are there and I'm here. I know when we see each other again, that will go away, but for now, what do I do? I go on in the name of the Lord, with your memories to sustain me and a determination to fulfill your legacy. You are my darling, my forever love.

These are the texts I sent to Terry's phone during my first two months without her. They reflect my feelings as I was and still am dealing with my grief. I'm up one day and down the next. Sometimes I'm all over the place in a single day, but in my pain, I'm never without hope. I can't give you an exact reason why texting Terry's phone is so important to me, but it is. People have told me, "You know she can't answer you back." I know that. But I can still talk to her, and I know she knows. I hope this helps you in some way.

9

WHEN TIME ISN'T ENOUGH

Psalms 78:39 – "He remembered that they were but flesh, a wind that passes and come not again."

Psalms 90:12 – "So teach us to number our days that we may get a heart of wisdom."

I REMEMBER WHEN I WAS YOUNG, older people would admonish me to "make good use of my time" and remind me that "time won't go on for-ever." Well, I didn't believe them for a minute, because I had so much time—so much that I could waste it if I wanted. They would also say that time speeds up when you get older, but to me, it was going at a snail's pace. Now, here I am on the other end of that argument, and I see that I was wrong.

As an old man, how can I say that my time with my beautiful wife wasn't enough? I mean, we had almost forty-nine wonderful years together. What do I want? More? Yes, I want more. How can I not? It was all so amazing, every single day. We never felt a day was wasted. Each day, we woke up, we loved each other, and we loved our life together. While we were enjoying today, we always looked forward to tomorrow.

Even for Christians who believe in life after death, there is not enough time to do everything in this life. Not enough time to be with people you love, not enough time to experience and learn, not enough time to even do things for the Lord. The Bible says that we must "number our days." Apostle Paul tells us to "redeem the time" or "buy up the opportunity." Even after doing all of this, no matter how long we have with a loved one, it isn't enough time.

Time isn't enough, but eternity will be enough. I will see Terry again, in a better place, and she will be healthy and happy, waiting for me with a big smile. She is with the Lord, along with her father and my mother and father, in that place reserved for all who died in the Lord.

In my grief, I have opened my broken heart to you. As you have walked with me while I have chatted about all of this, I pray that you have found something here in my meandering conversation to comfort you and help you as you heal. Healing does come, but it comes slowly.

The pain will always be there, but, gradually, you will realize that your life has purpose. Just remember that the more you help others, the better your life becomes. I hope you see that people need you and you need them.

Currently, I am still pastoring full time at the church and getting along with my life, while interacting with people. But no matter what I am doing, my thoughts are never far from my beloved wife.

I could literally go on and on about my beautiful, loving wife. My time with my darling Terry wasn't enough. But I hope I have given you a little peek into our life and what I have gone through as I have dealt with my grief. When she was first diagnosed, I bargained and negotiated with God for at least five more years. I held onto that hope until she became desperately sick, and then I pleaded for months, then weeks, then days, then hours, and finally minutes. When you lose the one you love, no amount of time is enough, but eternity is enough. I know that I will see Terry again, and we will pick up where we left off in a much better place.

Again, I will share that we were able to have a three-hour wake on Friday, an almost three-hour funeral on Saturday, a service dedicated to her on Sunday, and finally, her burial on Monday. God allowed me to celebrate her life for four days.

So many people, family and friends, helped me celebrate the life of a loving, godly woman who had a passion for helping people and extravagantly showed love to everyone she met, from immigrants to Muslims.

Terry loved everyone with the love of Christ. Just as she so persuasively and lovingly witnessed about her faith and her conversion in her letter to a beloved nephew, she lived her life as a witness. I tried to make that clear in my eulogy. I began by explaining that even though I am a preacher, I was not going to preach.

I was solely going to share the simple, powerful, loving life of faith in God that my wife lived. There would be no way people couldn't see Jesus Christ and His love through her life. And they did.

The Lord impressed on me to use Apostle Paul's epistle to the Galatians, in which Paul lists the fruit of the Holy Spirit, as a depiction of Terry's life in my eulogy. They are:

> *Gal 5:22-23 – "But the fruit of*
> *the Spirit is*
> *love,*
> *joy,*
> *peace,*
> *longsuffering,*
> *kindness,*
> *goodness,*

faithfulness,
gentleness,
self-control."

To me, Terry possessed all the fruit of the Spirit in her life, and she showed us how we should live daily as Christians. Her personality was always so sweet; it stood out in the world in which we are living today. As a young woman who studied history and politics in college, Terry just couldn't conceive the current rage in our wonderful country.

The vicious and terrible accusations coming from all sides on many different issues and the division it has all caused grieved her. She respected people's personal views and opinions, but she would often say, "How can we live our lives as Christians without the love of Christ? We must love and respect one another!"

As well informed as Terry was, she would never allow herself to be pulled into any political discussions, no matter what was going on in the news. Instead of getting angry or correcting people, she would just love them and pray for them. She would say, "Let's not listen to all of that. Let's just pray for everyone." I so admired that in her. God, help me to be more like her. No matter what's going on around me, always prompt me to show others the love of Christ. That's still the best answer.

Terry had a Christ-like spirit that she radiated every day of her life, which is what I tried to show to a church full of grieving people as I shared thoughts and memories from my broken heart at her funeral.

She also had a discipline I saw early in our relationship—a toughness to be good in everything. To see the best in everyone. To see the best in each other. An honesty to never let a night go by without making everything right with her husband. The quickness to always forgive and say, "I'm sorry." The laughs, the smiles, the hugs, just the touching of hands that assured me I was the most important person in the world to her.

She lived her life so that she never disappointed me, not once. I never knew of her disappointing anyone in her life, and best of all, she never disappointed anyone in our church. I don't know how she did it.

How was I so blessed to have her company for what I figure was 17,865 days? I don't have an answer to that, but I feel that I was blessed above all the men I have known. Our lifetime went by in a blink of an eye.

With these memories of Terry, I hope that God will help us all to live our lives like she did. I pray that He will give us the same encompassing love she had for everyone, that He will keep us from judging others we disagree with, like she did. God will help us to live out her legacy by becoming one in Christ.

At Terry's funeral, I bid her farewell at the close of my eulogy with these words: "Farewell, my angel. Farewell, my darling. I will see you in the morning when we walk, hand in hand, the streets of gold. When we rest our feet in the River of Life. We will dance around Heaven forever and ever."

With that, I was able to give her one last kiss, cover her in the casket, and then close it with my hand. The hand that had held hers for almost forty-nine years. When I turned to face the congregation, I realized that I would now walk this journey alone. But I haven't been alone; God has walked with me each day.

A couple of Sundays after Terry died, I preached from Psalms 30:5: "Weeping may endure for a night, but joy comes in the morning." I know that my weeping will continue as long as I live. Like me, you may have had many nights of grief and tears from your loss. That grief may cause you to question God and ask Him, "Why me?" I want you to know those questions will never diminish God's love for you. Your heart may be completely broken, your dreams shattered. And even though nothing will ever take the place of your loved one, God can bring you peace and joy in the morning. He will help you face another day.

Hold on to Him in prayer. Know that He cares. Remember the account of His disciples when they were in a terrible storm, the worst of their lives on the sea, as their little boat began to sink. The disciples questioned whether Jesus even cared about their predicament. Jesus did care, and He stood up and stilled the storm by saying, "Peace, be still." He is able to bring peace to your heart and life, no matter the storm. Just call on Him. He will comfort and console you because He loves you.

Though you may feel like it at times, don't give up on life. I know you may not feel the strength to press on right now — and this may sound trite — but your dark, stormy, and cloud-filled times will lead to days full of sunshine and blue skies. The sun will shine again. You will laugh again. And you will smile and remember all the wonders your loved one sowed into your life. After all, it was your life together that made you who you are. Your loved one wants you to go on.

Most of all, our loving heavenly Father still has a plan for your life. Be encouraged to go to Him in prayer and let Him guide your life. Your journey isn't finished, I promise; you have more living to do. In this new season, take the time to help others; it will strengthen you.

My life will go on because I am determined to finish the work my precious Terry started. I am going to continue loving God, continue loving people, and continue trying to change the world around me with the love of Jesus Christ. That was her legacy, and it is now my legacy.

Youthful Terry

Terry at one of her favorite places, the beach

Terry reading at the Bible Reading Marathon

Michael and Terry headed to the Opera

Michael and Terry at church

Michael and Terry reading together on the porch in
Massachusetts

Michael and Terry spending time together doing something they both loved, photography

WHO WILL PICK UP THE MANTLE

INTRODUCTION

IN *WHEN TIME ISN'T ENOUGH,* I SHARED THE
first part of the story about my late beloved wife, Terry
Shaffer Hall. This second part is about her Mantle, and
it honors this quiet, elegant woman who changed so
many lives. In this part of the story, I will share the
amazing love my wife and I had together and how this
love endured through a terrible battle with an aggressive cancer that eventually took her life.

Terry's death left me understanding how brief your
time, even almost forty-nine years, can be with a wonderful person you love. I'm still tracing my journey of
grief from her loss.

I continue to miss her more than words can convey.
At some point throughout each day, sitting in the little
house she rebuilt for us, the tears begin to fall. It's
not easy living my life without her, but looking back
on how she ministered with me, I realized she left an

incredible legacy. I continue trying to help the same people she always did. Sharing that part of her life helps me through my healing process as well.

I'm praying for the same strength Terry had so that I can continue to do what I feel God has planned for me in my remaining years. Part of that strength comes from going back through the well of our memories to reclaim what one loving woman did so effortlessly and so quietly that only in her death was most of it able to come to light. This is why I decided to write this second part about what I call Terry's Mantle.

If you never went to Sunday school, the term "mantle" may be obscure to you, but it was simply a piece of cloth originally worn in Old Testament times to ward off the cold. Sometimes it had a hole in the middle of it so a person could pull it over their head.

The Old Testament first mentions the mantle as a garment worn by Elijah and Elisha, as well as the prophet Samuel. But, in Elisha's case, the mantle took on a more important meaning. When Elijah's mantle had fallen off of him, Elisha picked it up, and it became his, an act symbolizing Elijah's ministry being passed on to Elisha.

Some theologians see the mantle as a symbol of the Holy Spirit and His anointing or of the prophets being wrapped in God's authority. However, if picking up the mantle symbolizes the carrying on of a ministry, I wanted to share a little about Terry's special Mantle in her ministry. And now that she is gone, I ask myself, who will carry on her ministry? Who will pick up her Mantle? Some of us? Maybe many of us, I hope.

Again, even if you are not religious, I still encourage you to read this. I know I have included quotes from the Bible, but as a pastor, that is the world in which I live. They are not here to offend you, but to provide direction. Terry was a special woman whose life touched everyone she met. In this part of her story, I have to delve a little deeper into her faith, as that is the core of why she did what she did. I can tell you that your life will be enriched by knowing more about her.

She Became an Important Part of a Special Church Family

Hebrews 10:24-25 – [24] *"And let us consider one another in order to stir up love and good works,* [25] *not forsaking the assembling of ourselves together, as is the manner of some, but exhorting one another, and so much the more as you see the Day approaching."*

Matthew 18:20 – "For where two or three are gathered together in My name, I am there in the midst of them."

Colossians 3:16 – "Let the word of Christ dwell in you richly in all wisdom, teaching and admonishing one another in psalms and hymns and spiritual songs, singing with grace in your hearts to the Lord."

WHEN TERRY BECAME A CHRISTIAN and started pouring over her Bible, she immediately wanted to become part of a church. Not surprisingly, she joined our church, The People's Church, a very special church on Capitol Hill. If she saw anything different about the church, as it had Caucasian pastors and a mostly African-American congregation, she never expressed it. The history of the church and how it came into existence fascinated her and was important to her when she came to work for the church. She wanted to know everything about its history. This made sense, because she thoroughly researched everything she got involved in.

I recounted that the founding pastors of this church, my parents, Pastor Fred W. Hall and Pastor Charlotte C. Hall, were originally from Texas. When they were newly married, they moved to California in 1940 to escape the effects of the Great Depression. There, God drew them to a wonderful Pentecostal church in Long Beach, California. My mother said the people there were so welcoming and wonderful that they wondered if that was what heaven would be like.

After they became Christians, my parents immediately started studying under the teaching and leadership of a great and godly man known for his passion for prayer and holiness, Pastor O.C. Harms. His powerful ministry was immersed in prayer and studying the Bible, and he passed this on to everyone he trained for the ministry.

After four years of studies and training, my mother and father were sent to pastor their first church in Redondo Beach, California, a beautiful town on the Pacific Coast, with the admonition to "live by faith." This meant they were sent out to establish a church without a single penny of support from the organization of which they were a part.

In Redondo Beach, they learned the old church planter's prayer of "praying in" every bit of food, every dollar of support, and every stick of lumber to build the church. They had no problem with this because they believed that God had called them to love people and preach the Gospel of Jesus Christ. They also reasoned that if God had called them, He would provide their needs; and as a result, their minimal needs were supplied.

Having moved from an insular all-Caucasian culture in Texas, they found themselves in the multi-cultural environment of Los Angeles, California. Far from seeing this as a negative, they were thrilled with the opportunity, for there, God first led them to minister across cultural and racial boundaries. The first step Pastor Fred Hall took to minister across racial lines was his outreach to the Mexican community in Long Beach. The next step was in the African-American community.

Around 1947, Pastors Fred and Charlotte Hall and their family visited Grace Memorial Church of God in Christ in West Los Angeles, an all African-American church, where they became friends with Bishop WJ Taylor. During this time, Pastor Hall and Bishop Taylor spent many hours discussing the segregation that was as obvious in the church as in society. In 1948, Pastor Hall, a Caucasian, and Bishop Taylor, an African American, took a bold step—they traded pulpits. Even though God moved mightily through both of these men's ministries, their denominations opposed such actions, which would be a subject of much discussion between these two pastors. Founding Pastor Fred Hall believed that through their ministries, God was demonstrating that His grace transcends everything.

During their time at that very first little church, WWII ended, and they began sending used clothes and books to people in Europe who were suffering. Even in those days, when they had few clothes, they would still go through the closets and share what they had.

The most amazing and special aspect of Founding Pastors Fred and Charlotte Hall's ministry was that from those early years and experiences, a seed was planted in Pastor Hall's heart. He said, "I know now what heaven is going to look like. It will be people from every nation, from every tribe, and we've been called to minister to them." He would instill that set of values in his own children. To this day, his children, Michael, Judy, Troyce, and Tony, all continue to practice those values.

From that point on, Pastor Fred and Charlotte asked God to use them to bring reconciliation by ministering to everyone that He brought across their path. Reconciliation became their vision; they would live their lives and model their ministry upon it. When I succeeded Pastor Fred as pastor of The People's Church, I vowed to continue that vision, and we have.

In 1949, my parents would pastor their second church in Santa Ana, California. It was in this church that God raised up a mighty group of young people, from which several were called into the ministry, and placed the second part of Pastor Hall's vision in place: "training ministers of the Gospel."

The following year, God miraculously gave their daughter, Judy Kay Hall, the gift of playing the piano and organ at the age of eight years old. She just sat down one day and played. Judy would later become the founding minister of music. For over six decades, her unusual gift of playing under the anointing has brought the sweet presence of the Lord into countless services. She has also mentored many successful organists through the years.

In those early years, the Hall family became friends with missionaries to Cuba and helped them by giving prayer, money, and clothes. These same missionaries then went to Africa, which opened up a whole new field of our mission giving.

In 1952, Fred and Charlotte planted another church, this time in Pacoima, California. They would pastor there until 1954, when God again called them into what they believed to be the "evangelistic field," which meant traveling around the country while conducting revival meetings and sharing the love of Jesus Christ.

For ten years, they traveled throughout the US, preaching in tents, auditoriums, and churches. It was a time of great revival in the land, which resulted in scores of people converting to Christ and lives completely changing.

Through their hours of praying and powerful preaching and teaching, countless lives were saved. Lives were changed through the power of God as Pastors Fred and Charlotte Hall poured themselves into the lives of others.

In the 1950s, God began to lead Pastor Hall to minister in the Native American community. Pastor Hall said he believed that God had given him and his family a wonderful calling and the opportunity to minister to people who did not look like us.

The People's Church began to take shape in Pastor Hall's heart in 1962. One day while in prayer, he felt God telling him to plant a church in Washington, DC. His church would be the second integrated church in the city.

With the answer to prayer about the church, Pastor Hall immediately shared the vision with Pastor Charlotte, and they quickly moved their family from California to Washington, DC.

In 1962, Washington, DC, was a divided city, noticeably segregated racially, economically, socially, and denominationally. It was obvious that this was a place in need of a church that would preach the message of reconciliation: the reconciliation between man and God and between man and man.

I don't know how they became so loving and accepting of so many different people, but I am proud of their commitment to minister that way.

After spending much time in the ministry observing racial and denominational separation in churches and church organizations, Pastor Fred and Charlotte vowed to someday pastor a church where everyone who walked through the doors would feel welcomed and loved.

In October of that year, they planted their church on Capitol Hill. Through the preaching of the Gospel of Jesus Christ, this church would become a soul-saving station, a hospital for wounded and hurting people, a restorer of families, a refuge for young people, and a training school for ministers.

Pastor Charlotte Hall suggested the name of the church—The People's Church—because of her great admiration of the missions-minded church in Canada, also called The People's Church. This name would welcome everyone who came into this sanctuary.

The People's Church also reflected their ministry, which, since the 1940s, had taken a stand against the unbiblical actions of racism, segregation, and separation. God had called this ministry into existence to be effective in ministering to everyone.

Since the beginning of The People's Church, Pastor Fred and Charlotte decided to put into practice the belief that no matter your race—African American, Caucasian, Hispanic, Asian, Indian, Native American— no matter your political party, no matter your lifestyle, you would be welcome to come into the church and hear the Gospel of Jesus Christ. From 1962 to 1992, the church watched as scores of people became devout Christians, were delivered from destructive lifestyles, and were established in the kingdom of God.

Many young people grew up in the church and were called into the ministry. Church members and visitors were encouraged to attend college and purchase homes — and all this inspiration came from an unusual, vibrant, and thriving church planted on Capitol Hill.

In 1992, as his health was failing, Pastor Fred Hall requested that his son, Michael Hall, who had been studying, training, and working in the ministry, succeed him as senior pastor of The People's Church. In August of that year, after battling five years of illness, Founding Pastor Fred Hall was called home to the eternal reward he so richly deserved.

My wife, Terry, immediately embraced the vision of the church and began pouring her love into everyone she met. She was determined that we carry on the founding pastors' mission to change people's lives by loving them and teaching them to pray and study God's Word; to witness, to worship, and to live holy lives according to biblical principles; and to show God's love to everyone.

Terry's joy of being a Christian was infectious. She believed that by our witness in the world, we can change the world around us, and she understood from God's Word that we are to be Salt and Light. The quiet person that she was, she would remark that salt and light make no sound, but they certainly change things around them.

She embraced the calling of this church to minister the love of God through the simplicity of the Gospel of Jesus Christ. As long as Terry lived and worked with me in the ministry, she understood the mission to continue to train the next generation and to train ministers and spiritual leaders. She was a tireless helper to everyone.

Terry prayed that the power of the Holy Spirit would be manifest in the lives of believers and in the church. By example, she showed the love of Christ to everyone who came through the front doors of the church, demonstrating that this church exists to minister the love of Jesus Christ through the Gospel, the life-changing Word of God, and the power of the Holy Spirit.

It was clear to Terry that we had picked up the Mantle for loving everyone from my parents. Even before this terrible time of division, she could see that not everyone agreed with her view, but that didn't matter to her. She loved working in this special church because she herself was so special. The wonderful thing about our church is that we are not divided. We are one in Christ, and we have found a wonderful unity in Him. We truly are a family.

Terry loved my late father's heart for overseas missions and helping so many different people. Her heart for giving toward missions knew no bounds, and she made sure we came alongside established Christian ministries around the world. Most of our giving went and still goes to Africa, but we didn't stop there; Terry insisted that we give as much as we can to local mission outreaches. As this country began to become less Christian, more biblically illiterate, and less inclined to worship in churches of whatever size, Terry felt the mission field here in America was growing. We wanted to reach this generation with the love of Christ. They need it.

Shortly before she died, Terry and I talked about how our family has had the honor and privilege of working with people of color for over seventy years. I asked her if she noticed that in this day, some Christians have again begun to feel that we should only minister to and work with people just like us. For some reason, the fact that we don't makes some of them uncomfortable.

She would say, "Oh Michael, don't worry about that. Think of the joy and privilege we have in doing what we do. Look at the beautiful people in our church that God has allowed us the honor of serving. We are fulfilling the words of Christ. Just love them and pray for those people who take exception to what we are doing. Think of what they are missing. It's their loss." She was right.

What a joy it was for her to pour her love into young people who I think will now pick up her torch and carry on for their generation. Terry never despaired about young people, and she was always so excited about their potential. She would remind so many of us that you can go back even as far as ancient Greek writings to find accounts of older people worrying about youth that sound just like elders today. And yet, here we are. Terry had complete confidence in this scripture:

> *Proverbs 22:6 – "Train up a child in the way he should go: and when he is old, he will not depart from it."*

> *Proverbs 22:6 (NLT) – "Direct your children onto the right path, and when they are older, they will not leave it."*

We live out this scripture by showing Christ's love through His Gospel and The Holy Bible, which is God's Word to us. Even with my devastating loss of my wife, I can look back and say that every day, we were glad to be part of a church family that is determined to go on together. Even though we are different, we are so alike in our love of Christ and each other. Being witnesses to the world has made all of us brothers and sisters in

Christ, and we have the joy of bearing one another's burdens, as the Bible commands us to do.

SOMETIMES IT COMES DOWN TO JUST BEING FAITHFUL

Proverbs 28:20 – "A faithful man will abound with blessings…"

1 Corinthians 4:2 – "Moreover it is required in stewards that one be found faithful."

Luke 16:10 – "He who is faithful in what is least is faithful also in much…"

THE WORD "FAITHFUL" MEANS LOYAL, full of faith and trust, firmly and resolutely staying with a person, a group, a cause, a belief, or an idea, without waver. Terry understood that we at The People's Church are neither famous, nor important, nor powerful; we are a small church, just one little part of God's great kingdom. But to be an important little part, we must be faithful.

In the Old Testament, there is a story of a warrior named Shamma, one of King David's mighty men. The top two mighty men were incredible warriors who were famous for their amazing exploits in battle. Shamma's claim to fame was defending a small lentil patch against an army of Philistines. Somehow, this battle, this one small act, brought an important victory to ancient Israel—so important that King David listed Shamma as one of the three most significant military leaders who ever fought with him.

Afterward, Shamma may have wished to be famous for doing something bigger and grander, but God chose him for that one small job. And he was faithful in doing exactly what he was asked to do. Sometimes, just being faithful in doing the right thing, no matter how small it may seem to you or others, is all it takes. Small things can be very important. Far beyond what we can imagine. Terry did many important things in her life, but she was always faithful in pouring love into people, especially those whom others did not particularly love.

Among the many people whose lives she touched, Terry latched onto an older man on the street who had been around forever. She kept telling him that he was going to give his life to Christ and God would help him get his life together, and he did. Another lady, who had ended up working the streets and was battling AIDS, became a Christian and a member of our church. Terry would wrap her arms around this woman and tell her how inspiring her worship and dance before the Lord was.

Always, Terry would look for ways to reach out and help people who were different from us. She would say, "What if people don't look like us? What if people are not like us? Does it matter that people are different? That makes it all the more interesting, and it fulfills the Great Commandment of Christ, who said, 'Go into all the world, and preach the Gospel to everyone.'"

There are big, powerful churches and religious organizations that have access to vast amounts of money and scores of people. Some of them have great power and authority, and some are connected to the most influential of political people. But Terry felt that many small groups, or even individuals, were mistaken if they felt they couldn't do great things for God. Jesus Himself worked with a small group. She believed that if you were genuine, being small was never a detriment to building the kingdom of God. Sometimes, those acts that are small in the eyes of men are the most important ones in God's eyes.

We always felt we were blessed to live here in the Washington, DC, metro area, where we have had the privilege of ministering in an international city with people from every corner of the world. With all the arguing and fighting over immigrants today, it's interesting that people from all over the world have been in our country since its founding. We always thanked God for the opportunity to minister in this incredible mission field. After all, it has afforded us the privilege of meeting Christians from almost every country. In this field, we have found that the message of the Gospel of Jesus Christ—the message of hope and love—works regardless of who you are or where you are from.

Terry and I never understood why people are reluctant to get involved with other cultures, when immersing yourself in another culture doesn't mean that you lose your own. We loved doing it. She would say, "It's not only biblical; it is exciting." Terry was a strong believer in the Great Commission that Christ gave us. Throughout her life, she maintained and demonstrated daily that our faith is a muscular and robust one. It does just fine in the marketplace and can stand up to anything. And it has.

In her spiritual walk, Terry always hoped that people would look a little closer at the one verse in the Bible that almost everyone knows and loves—*John 3:16*. This beloved scripture says, *"For God so loved the world that He gave His only begotten Son and whoever believes in Him shall not perish, but, have everlasting life."* She would say, "Notice this verse doesn't say, 'For God loved just the US,' or 'loved just England,' or 'loved just Africa,' or 'loved just Israel,' or 'loved just South America,' or 'loved just any other country.' God so loved the world."

Within our ministry, one aspect of the Gospel of Jesus Christ that we focus on is the fact that the Gospel knows no national boundaries. We can take it to everyone on this little planet. After all, this is the only planet that we know is inhabited, and it is getting smaller all the time. So, while we are being grateful that we are Americans, let us not forget that, even more importantly, we are Christians as well.

This was Terry's walk of faithfulness every day— her walk of rightness. She had the determination to be the same every day, to always look for someone suffering in this country or other countries who she could help. In her great love, Terry wanted to let them know that they were not alone in their battle and that she could and would help them. She would do all of this while ensuring that we lived a life full of adventure almost every day.

She loved the following verses:

> *John 17:20-21 – "I do not pray for these alone, but also for those who will believe in Me through their word;* [21] *that*

they all may be one, as You, Father, are in Me, and I in You; that they also may be one in Us, that the world may believe that You sent Me."

Romans 12:16 (NLT) – "Live in harmony with each other. Don't be too proud to enjoy the company of ordinary people. And don't think you know it all!"

Terry was an educated woman who read voraciously, always studied, and voted in local and national elections. She was a political science major in college, although she cared little about politics, and she loved her country and her neighborhood.

She would say, "First, I'm thankful to be a citizen of heaven. Second, I'm thankful to be a citizen of the body of Christ, worldwide, and third, I'm thankful to be a citizen of America, in that order."

Often, she would add, "Even though I'm a citizen of heaven and not of this earth, I am living here, so as a Christian, I must make everything and everyone around me better through my life."

Also, as I stated earlier, Terry loved moving into old houses and fixing them up—just like how she married an older man and fixed him up. She fixed up everything that needed fixing—people, situations, and anything else were all fertile fields for her to sow love and unity.

As I pick up what I'm calling her Mantle, I think the path of rightness that Terry strived to walk as a Christian each day sets an example for all of us. I loved hearing her say in situations, "This is just the right thing to do," and then watch her do it.

I was also impressed at her ability to somehow stay out of all the shouting and disagreeing going on. She would make it a point to never insult or demean anyone, even those whose views were opposite to hers, while working to bring people together, rather than divide them. Likewise, she absolutely believed that God unites us while the Devil divides us, and she simply refused to judge others on their life or their views.

If you protect and fight for the precious people who are the very ones under attack in this highly political and racially divisive time, your service will bring you under attack as well. Even though she didn't have a fighting bone in her body—and I have many—Terry would fight for the disenfranchised, the down, and the outer. But, somehow, in all of this, she managed to love everyone on all sides of the issues. This takes a strong love. A love that is able to overlook. A love that the Bible says *"covers a multitude of sins."*

Before she died, Terry was sad that even people of faith were willingly dividing themselves on current issues of the day. She asked me, "Why do they scramble around the floor looking for crumbs when they can set a banquet of God's love and His Word before a hurting and lost world?" She would smile and continue, "Oh well, this can be fixed." And then she would begin building bridges. After, she would look at me and say, "See what a little love can do." This was how she looked at everything. She knew how to get around obstacles that stopped everyone else by doing something loving, something positive, something constructive.

This gift for achieving the impossible was visible in her life as a planner, a worker, a fixer, a forgiver, a cheerleader, and a dispenser of much needed love and godly, practical wisdom. She was good at taking the long view without getting bogged down and overly discouraged by daily problems. She had the ability to see the bigger picture. Before we decided to do anything, she would say that we needed to think and look and act like God wants us to. She knew how to leave it in His hands.

As a Matter of Fact, I Am Still Texting Terry

Yes, I'm still talking to my wife through texts to her. As I explained in the first part of this book, it helps me deal with my grief, for it reminds me of our wonderful life together and keeps her alive to me. If the one you love is still alive, treasure every minute you have with them, because when they are gone, you will realize that each minute was precious. If you have lost your loved one, relive the memories; it can help. If you are a person of faith, God will help you through this.

Friday, July 19th, 9:50 p.m.

Goodnight, my darling. No matter how long I live, I will miss you every night of my life. Miss the nearness of you. Miss holding your hand and just being with you. Often, we didn't have to talk or have music or the TV on. There was such enjoyment in our silence. Then a look and a smile. Without a word, we would commu-nicate with each other. Not even death can break that bond. Our hearts are still intertwined, and they will be forever. Love you so.

Saturday, July 20th, 8:24 a.m.

Good morning, my sweet Terry. We're in the middle of a heat wave. So, I'm staying indoors when it's hottest. Going to ride the Trike over to your mom's this morning before it gets too hot. She wants two of your leather coats. Those two are special to her because she remem-bers buying them for you and how happy you were. You never asked for or wanted anything. You were always so unselfish. Always concerned about others. You were an amazing woman, and I was always madly in love with you. Our love endures.

Oh, Lord, I miss my precious wife so. I'm getting ready for my ninth Sunday without her. The emptiness I feel is overwhelming. Sitting here looking at the water, her favorite view, tears are streaming down my cheeks. The house is silent, the neighborhood is quiet, and I'm longing for the sound of her voice, her steps. The greatest singer in the world's voice is not as beautiful as her just talking to me. I'm longing for her. God, You said in Your Word that You are close those of us who have a broken heart. Thank You.

Saturday, July 20th, 6:24 p.m.

Closing out a hot Saturday. If the pain of losing you is this intense in warm weather, what will winter be like? I will always grieve for you. I will always wish I could have done more for you. I will from now on be an injured shepherd, who walks with a noticeable limp. I wonder if every time Jacob limped in pain he remembered. I'm sure he did. I know that every step I take from here forward will be steps in pain. It's late in the day; everything is quiet and lonely without you my darling. The Bay is calm and blue, even in this heat. I can see it through my tears. If I could only hold you in my arms and tell you how much I love you. When you were sick, I couldn't let myself think about losing you. I was just doing everything I could to keep you well and alive. It's so much worse than I feared.

If couples only knew the pain they would feel after a loved one dies, they would treasure every minute of every day together. Until it happens, they can't imagine how quickly their life together will go by. And then, in a flash, it will be over. No possible way of bringing it back. No would have, should have…it's gone. Your life together is gone. You will have to have confidence in God then. He is the only One who can comfort and console you. Oh, God, be our comfort, please. Why can't I look at a picture of you without breaking down in tears? Will I ever come to a place of joy for what we had? Every part of our life together was wonderful. How can that be? Every hour of every day. How blessed by God we were. I guess every time I look at your picture, it all rushes back. Oh, Terry, my darling, why did I have to lose you? Your mom said that you would be just as broken up losing me. But I'm the oldest by far. Why didn't I go first? I want to be with you. Just a few years, and I will see you again.

Sunday, July 21st, 11:01 a.m.

Well, it's time for church to start, and I haven't text you yet. So miss you being with me at church. Such an empty feeling without you. Will talk to you later.

Sunday, 5:41 p.m.

Don't know why I was so mixed up this morning. But eventually, I felt like you were trying to get me in gear to go to church ahead of time. And so, I did. I prayed with you, as I do before I leave for service. That God would protect us on our journey. You can see I still feel like your presence is with me. And that God would make us a blessing to whoever He wants. And I feel that He did today. But again, I missed having you with me in church. I can never tell you enough how important your influence on me being a pastor was. If I do anything worthwhile for the kingdom of God, you make me who I am. Thank you, my precious wife.

Sunday, 8:12 p.m.

Well, day is closing. Another Sunday without you. It is the Lord's Day; we should rejoice and be glad in it, as Scripture says. I'm hoping for some healing for my broken heart so that I can rejoice for all that you mean to me. Even though I'm going on alone, it will always be we. It will always be Terry and Michael. Not even death can separate us. When I preached today, you were there preaching with me. It was just the kind of sermon you would encourage me to preach. "What must I do to be saved?" About coming to Jesus. Thank you for your input.

Monday, July 22nd, 7:52 a.m.

Good morning, my beautiful darling. Just reworking a couple of pages in my tribute to you. I want so desperately to honor you. You never understood how special you were. I know, and I'm going to spend the rest of my life making sure as many people as possible know as well. You will live on in the minds and lives of so many. Because of that, you will continue to change lives. Isn't that amazing?

Monday, 5:57 p.m.

Late afternoon. Trying at last to pay some bills. Trying to get my mind and my life organized. I feel like I have been in such a fog the last months of your life. And especially after you died. Trying to get back to normal, my "new normal" without you. Pastor Stratton has been such a blessing sharing what it was like losing her sister. She pointed out how short people's comfort and pity is. And I know they can't help it. Life can't be all about comforting me, and I wouldn't want that anyway. Life moves on, regardless. Speaking of life moving on, such awful political times we are living in. You would be so sad at how terrible the news is on every side. There is no civility, no honesty, no respect, and no compassion anywhere. I wish normal working people would just ignore all these terrible people on every side of every issue. I'm also so sad and ashamed of what we have become as a country. We need a national spiritual revival. I'm so glad that our citizenship is in a country whose builder and maker is God Himself. In the meantime, as I'm waiting to join you, my darling, let me be a blessing to someone in need.

My darling, my darling. Why wasn't I able to have more time with you? As much as you worked and planned for us to have many later years together, it didn't work out that way, and my heart is broken now, never to be repaired. I sit in our little house by the Bay, so often at the close of the day, missing you so desperately. Just trying to look again at the view we both loved, but my eyes are so often filled with tears. I'm just empty and so diminished without you. Why are you not here with me? I need you. I miss you every minute of every single day. I guess it will be this way till I see you again, my precious love. The only comfort I get is from helping others. God, help me to do that.

Monday, 9:47 a.m.

Goodnight, my darling. One of those up-and-down days. What do you think about how I'm handling everything? I want to make you proud. But I don't have you, and I'm a shadow of myself without you. Just know this: this half a person is still madly in love with you. Goodnight, my love.

Tuesday, July 23rd, 8:16 a.m.

Good morning, my love. Rainy summer day. Humid, but much cooler. Just a little break from the summer heat. Dreamed one of those crazy dreams on not being prepared. Supposed to preach somewhere; can't find anything I'm looking for in the old Bible I'm carrying. Not a single note, and my iPhone is jammed. I get up to speak, everyone is waiting, and my mind is a blank. Yikes! I know it's my brain trying to tell me to get better organized. I'm trying; honestly, I am. There is no better example than you. Just a couple of weeks before you died, you organized our pictures. Otherwise I wouldn't have found those beautiful pictures of you and me.

Tuesday, 2:00 p.m.

Ok, midafternoon. Home to chill for a little while, waiting for lingering showers to stop so I can work in the shed. Put some chrome shelves together for the house and the shed, and need to start getting my tools out of the house and into the shed. In a tiny house, extra room is measured in inches. Wish you were here to advise me.

Tuesday, 9:22 p.m.

Goodnight, sweetheart. Wish I had done more around the house when you were here. I'm doing it now for your memory. Even with all the mess and work as I'm making more storage room, it's empty and quiet. And when I say that, I mean that no one can ever or ever will take your place. Your legacy will live on. Your work will go on.

You will live on; I'm going to see to that. That probably embarrasses you, but you were a masterpiece. God only made one copy, and He blessed me with you. I love you.

Wednesday, July 24th, 7:47 a.m.

Good morning, my dear, loving wife. I sit in my chair at the beginning of everyday and wish for you. Saddened that the dreams we made together won't be fulfilled here. This morning, I'm headed to Summer Camp at the church for a little while, then to have lunch with Mark. I will place in his capable hands my small book honoring you. If I had your skills, it would be so much better. It's just the thoughts from my broken heart. I'm hoping and praying that somehow it can be printed, so I can get it into the hands of people to show how special you were. I love you.

Wednesday, July 24th, 9:33 p.m.

Goodnight, my darling. Don't know why I'm so exhausted; must be old age, ha. I love you so much and miss you more than words can describe. Every time I'm around our friends, it should help, but it just reminds me of losing you. Just a few years here, and then I'll be there with you. Can't wait.

Thursday, July 25th, 6:59 a.m.

A very sad day for me. Two months since I lost you. Yes, I'm keeping track of the days. How can I not? To wake up to a day without your beautiful, loving smile. To not hear your voice. Oh, what I would give just to listen to you talk, about anything. To see you walking toward me, knowing that you would be in my arms. Just to go anyplace at all with you would be the greatest gift. I miss you so much.

You were everything to me. Do you know that? I'm even keeping little shopping lists you made, just to look at your handwriting. You know, I cry every morning when I first sit in my chair and look at the Bay from the comfortable little house you rebuilt for us. Every single day, I sit waiting for you to come in and have breakfast so we can get on with our day. All of our days together started well and ended well. We never went to bed angry or got up angry. What a treasure.

Thursday, 7:25 p.m.

Wow! What a day. I'm whipped! Got all the new shelves and all my tools in the shed, and I can fit my Trike as well.

Thursday, 9:33 p.m.

Goodnight, my sweet darling. I guess the best thing for me to do is keep busy. It makes time go faster, which ultimately will get me to you. When I'm riding my Trike, I look up into the heavens and wonder if you can see me. Are you watching over me? I hope so. I want to make you proud of me. Hoping the little book I wrote about you is a blessing to many people. I think there might be another one in me, maybe. I know I have so much more to say about you. I love you so much.

Friday, July 26th, 7:47 a.m.

Good morning, sweetheart. Going to go to church and encourage the wonderful volunteers who have worked so hard with the kids for two weeks of Summer Camp. You always loved what they did. Somehow, I have to get Theresa and James to get some rest. So wish you were going with me today. Love you, my darling.

Friday, 6:30 p.m.

Ok, early Friday evening. Ralph's coming down so we can ride around locally. We'll see. He's a lot braver than me. I think you're keeping me safe by me riding carefully.

Friday, 9:22 p.m.

Well, we went to Deale for sushi. I got the cooked stuff, so it was good. Enjoying my Trike, but so lonely for you, no matter what I'm doing. I talk to you and the Lord when I ride. I do enjoy being close to nature but wish I could share it with you. It's Friday night, early, and all I want to do is go to bed. Without you, everything is empty. You filled everything in my life with joy; now you are gone, so how can I ever be happy? The only joy in my life will be doing the Lord's work, which I will do the rest of my life, and be a blessing to my family. Thinking about a second little book about your Mantle. Goodnight, my darling.

Saturday, July 27th, 9:10 a.m.

My darling, my darling. It's Saturday; tomorrow will be my 10th Sunday in this year of firsts without you. Each first will be sad. Do you know how much you mean to me?

Saturday, 9:22 a.m.

Good evening. Sorry, it seems like 20 Sundays, but tomorrow will be my 10th Sunday without you. Went for a long ride to VA and back down to So. MD with Ralph today. Too much for an old man. We'll just do short jaunts, mostly around here. This walk without you is a lonely walk. I need spiritual support so desperately. You were always rock steady. I know you are present in spirit. Goodnight, my beautiful, darling wife. I have one of your old t-shirts you slept in.

Sunday, July 28th, 6:44 a.m.

Good morning, my precious. It is the Lord's Day. It is also my 10th Sunday without you. So, the half of me that's left will go to church and encourage the young people.

Sunday, 7:51 a.m.

Getting ready for church. Just love being in church and worshipping God. We were together in our faith. I think we strengthened each other. The feeling of your presence and your memories continue to inspire me to go on serving God. I love you. How do we stop this division that is spreading through this country, my Terry?

Sunday, 7:09 p.m.

I don't have to ask what you would say about stopping the division in this country. If we would use your life as an example. Be nice to everyone. Don't call people bad names. Respect people, even if they disagree with you. Play fair. Oh, that's right, you said you learned that when you were a little kid. I guess a lot of people never learned those lessons or grew up. Thanks for always being you.

Sunday, 9:18 p.m.

Goodnight, my love. Sorry about my last text. Hope you don't think I was going after anyone in particular. I really wasn't, and I want to be a shepherd to everyone I can. You taught me that. Thank you.

Monday, July 29th, 8:07 a.m.

Good morning, love. Thinking of all I wished I had talked to you about. We talked so freely about everything, I thought, but here I am, finding myself with questions. But this is all set up so that you can't answer me directly. Gotta tell you, after almost 49 years, I don't think that's fair. Not one bit. I need your wisdom. I need your always sound advice. I need you. I know someday, when I'm with you, I'll understand, but right now, I miss you desperately.

Monday, 2:42 p.m.

Early, sticky summer afternoon. That time of the year. Can't take the heat like I could when I was younger. Pretty funny. I'm the one who always loves hot weather and complained about freezing weather; now, both extremes bother me. Whatever the weather, it was always fun with you.

Tuesday, July 30th, 8:17 a.m.

Goodnight, my dear. A lonely day without you. Sometimes, I feel like retreating into our little house for days at a time. Having a hard time fitting into everyone's normal life. I don't fit in; that's the problem. I know there is a purpose for my life. But without you, I don't know. I guess time will make some things a little better. We will see.

Well, that was something. Wrote a text to you last night and forgot to send it till this morning. I am slipping. Good morning, beautiful wife. I miss you today.

Sitting here in my chair looking at the fireplace you had Pastor Alvarez build. It brought you so much joy in the winter. I can see you building a fire in it, a smile on your face every time. I spend most of my time in this room because it reminds me of you, my darling. I miss you so much today. Don't know how long I can make it without you. Not that I'm giving up on life, but no matter what I do, or who I'm with, it's so empty without you. Yes, I'm making a few new experiences on my Trike, but they are empty as well. You were not only a huge part of my life; you were my life. I guess it's a little like losing a limb, only more so. Life goes on, but it's strange, it's hard, it's difficult, and it's certainly not the same, and it never can be again. This is my journey. This is when I need my Shepherd to come along side of His injured and crippled sheep and help him. And He does help me, outwardly and inwardly. For that I am grateful.

Tuesday, 8:89 p.m.

Goodnight, sweet Terry. I'm glad I have so many wonderful memories to walk with me in this lonely journey. The Lord is my Shepherd, and you are with me as well. Knowing that this journey ends with you not too many years from now sustains me. I will continue our ministry together. I will try to bring peace where there is strife. I will try to bring unity where there is division. And I will show the love of Jesus Christ to everyone I meet. Love you. I feel you impressing me not to worry about things that don't concern me. Just keep my eyes on the Cross. Thank you, my love.

Wednesday, July 31st, 8:45 a.m.

Good morning, my love. Miss you. Want you to come to me in my dreams, please.

Wednesday, 2:17 p.m.

Well, after working on part two of your little book, I decided to ride over to Dunkirk to Chipotle's for lunch. Then way on down to my Harley place in Hughsville to pick up an antenna. And talk to them about some modifications I want them to make at the 1000-mile mark. Back to the grocery store and drug store and then home. Going to chill a while before service tonight. My knees are giving me fits. Must be the humidity. Just bringing you up to date on my day. What's happening where you are? Wish you could share that with me. Love you.

Wednesday, 9:33 p.m.

Back from church and ready for bed. Shed some tears in prayer before service, thinking about you and wishing you were with me in church. It's a lonely walk now. Small crowd. The speaker didn't show up, so I spoke for a few minutes, then Elder Moore and then Rev. Ferguson finished. It was good, thank the Lord. Thank goodness for God's mercy and His presence. Miss you so much, my darling. Hope I see you in my dreams.

Thursday, August 1st, 8:50 am.

Well, a late good morning to you, my darling. Life has moved on for everyone around me, but I'm still stuck in this place that I'm in. Missing you every day.

Wanting to see you, hold you, kiss you, and talk to you. Will my life be one of an old man ever grieving over the loss of his wife? I don't know how it can be anything else. But I'm grateful for the time we had together. My memory is filled with so many stories of our life. Love you.

Friday, August 2nd, 7:19 a.m.

Wow! I only text you once yesterday. I guess it was because I was talking and writing so much about you. So many things I want to share with people about you. You will continue to have an impact on lives. I'll see to that.

It's a rainy summer day. Have to decide what to do today. I think I have to rework my message a little. I love you, my darling. You did come to me briefly in my dreams. Thank you.

I think it's the aloneness—of what, the loss of my wife and old age? Really, my life is good, for someone my age. I'm employed. I'm able to live by myself, with my cat looking after me. So, I'm not complaining about my lot in life. Life is good. I'm still able to be a blessing to people; I just have to find the joy of my past, so it can outweigh the grief. With God's help, I'm marching in that direction. I'm thankful He can still use me. All because of you, my love.

Friday, 9:26 a.m.

I guess I'm going through some of, and maybe all of, the stages of grief that a loved one supposedly feels losing their spouse. It really is up and down daily. The pain of loss will always be there to some extent, I imagine. With God's grace and help, it will even out in time, I hope. I do enjoy sitting here in our little house alone, thinking about you. Reliving wonderful memories. Do you think about me?

Friday, 10:35 a.m.

Oh, my beautiful Terry. I love you more than life itself. Every single day with you was a treasure. You were a treasure. No one like you, ever. How was I so blessed to have you in my life? My precious love for time and eternity.

I am the most blessed of all men, that you chose to spend your life with me. I'm going to do my best to carry on your legacy of love, prayer, and doing for others. God help me to be half as good as you were. I haven't isolated myself from people or life, but sometimes, I just need to be alone with you.

Thank you, Lord, for not letting me be afraid to be alone. With my thoughts and my memories and you, I am not really alone, although at times, it seems I am. Looks like I'm making up for yesterday.

Saturday, August 3rd, 6:58 a.m.

Good morning, my love. My texting is getting herky jerky. Sorry. First Saturday prayer. You always enjoyed that simple little prayer meeting. Just waiting in His presence, asking for His direction for the month. I certainly need to talk to Him today. This is my 3rd month without you. Hasn't gotten any easier, my darling. Nothing fills the big hole you left. Memories of you and our life help, of course, but I miss you so.

Every morning, when I sit in my chair with my breakfast of whole wheat toast with Irish butter and a protein drink, I give thanks. First, for the day, then my salvation, and then you, and then I cry. Every time. I know the Bible says that where you are, God will wipe away all your tears; I hope so, because here, they still come every day.

Saturday, 6:07 p.m.

I need your help, my darling. Messing up so many things on my phone and computer. Yikes!

Saturday, 9:22 p.m.

Well, my darling, here is my dilemma: everything around me is pretty much back to normal, except me. I'm a widower without his beautiful wife now. How do I continue on with my diminished and sad life? Sometimes I wonder what there is to live for. Every moment of the day, I want to be with you. Everything I experience, I want to share with you, but I can't. And no one but me can understand that. But, for the Lord's sake, my family's sake, and my church's sake, I need a few more years to finish my task. Then the Lord can take me home to be with Him and my sweet Terry. I know the Bible says our times are in His hands. He alone knows the time of our departure. So, I'll leave it to Him. Goodnight, my darling. I missed you today. You are always in my thoughts.

Sunday, August 4th, 7:28 a.m.

Good morning, my darling. So grateful for all that you did for me when you were here, and what you did to make sure I would be alright if you were not here. What an incredibly loving wife you are. I love you.

Sunday, 10:10 a.m.

Have to leave earlier because of the traffic. First time I can remember that I was not early on Sunday morning.

Thank goodness, Brittany was here to open up. I do miss you on Sundays. You were such an important part of Lord's Day worship.

Sunday, 4:51 p.m.

Ok, home with the cat. Just the two of us, thinking about you. Missing you so much. What is it like there? Do you pray? Have you seen your father and my folks? How are they? It must be amazing to be absent from the body and present with the Lord. I can't wait, but I will wait till my job is done. We sing that old hymn, "I Need Thee Every Hour," and that is how I feel about you, my love.

Sunday, 9:36 p.m.

My darling. I'm so glad that we both came to know the Lord. That we both served Him together so many wonderful years. Because of that, we will spend eternity together. Isn't that wonderful? I think you are whispering that to me to encourage me. Oh, the joy you brought me. Let me hang onto that joy and have the opportunity to share Christ with others. May my Trike open up a new mission field for me. Whenever I ride, I take the Lord and you with me. I can feel your presence with me. Thank you, my love, and goodnight.

Monday, August 5th, 8:12 a.m.

Good morning, my precious. That must be amusing to you, since there is no night where you are. Do you remember what it was here? I hope so. What does the concept of time seem like to you? I'm plugging along in time down here, slowed by a constantly aging, earthly body. But my love for you is eternal.

Monday, 9:31 a.m.

What to do to stop the feeling that I'm dying little by little every day without you. A picture, a piece of clothing, so many things remind me of you, and I just start crying. I don't want to put this heavy, dark feeling on family and friends because there is no way they could understand. And they certainly don't deserve it for all the comfort they have extended to me. I'm never giving up, but it is a struggle every day without you. Nothing makes me happy. You are the only one who could do that. So, I miss that.

Monday, 9:37 p.m.

Ok. What a day. Over to Kent Island with Justin, Cynthia, and Judy. Crabs and seafood. First time without you. It was a job to stay happy. All I could think about was you. We went a lot of places together. All fun. Came back home, and Judy helped Cynthia find shoes, boots, and clothes from your collection. She was happy, and I'm happy that you live on in her life. Miss you, my darling.

Tuesday, August 6th, 6:35 a.m.

Good morning, my love. Well, I'm going to Orphans Court this morning to give your mom support. Your mom's late husband's daughter has hauled her into court to try and get some of the little money Jim left your mom. For all that she did being his round-the-clock nurse, especially the last five years, and his daughter and grandkids doing practically nothing, it's awful. They hardly ever came to see him. I know because of how disappointed he was, and we were there. Don't understand that level of nastiness. I guess she's not taking into account the money your mom spent on her dad's house, or the car your mom gave her, or the money that she prevailed on Jim to give her and her kids.

I just feel so bad for your mom. She is so upset and doesn't need this kind of harassment at 88. I'm praying for God's protection for your mom. I'll look out for her, I promise. Love you so much. I think I may understand his daughter's attack on your mom. It seems to be a lack of gratefulness and thankfulness to people who are good to you. That is sad. And God forgive me for judging her. I've noticed that people who are neither grateful nor thankful are usually unhappy people.

You were always so grateful and thankful, and you were always happy. That's one reason life was so good with you and good to people who were around you.

Tuesday, 9:41 a.m.

Wow! Your mom's case was dismissed. Thank you, Lord. Having a late breakfast with your mom and Mickie.

Tuesday, 8:07 p.m.

I am again looking at the Bay, thinking about your battle with cancer. Beginning in September, I got to take you to MV 7 straight months in a row. I'm thankful that we got to go together and spend time there. But why did I not see how fast you were losing ground? I know I did almost everything I could do for you. But if I had known, I would have done more. Oh, my darling, I miss you every single day; I miss you terribly. I know you are with the Lord, and I'm glad about that, but I'm just so lonely for you.

Tuesday, 10:25 p.m.

Goodnight, my darling. No matter how many years I live, there will never be a night I don't long to go to sleep in our bed with you. I miss you so. I love you forever.

Wednesday, August 7th, 8:47 a.m.

A late good morning, my love. As I sit here, like I always do in the mornings, my thoughts turn directly to you. I have finally moved over to the sofa. Right by where you were in your hospice bed. I know you loved that big coffee table, but I can't put it back here. It's almost sacred ground to me. I have a picture of your hand in my hand. Everything about your beautiful body seemed so healthy; just can't believe you were so sick. What I would give to hold your hand again. So hard to text through tears.

Wednesday, 3:11 p.m.

Early afternoon. Just back from the church and getting ready for tonight. Patrick got all the grass and weeds pulled in front where the flowers are. You would be so happy. Flowers are like you; they bring joy to people and smiles to their face. Everything that brings real joy to people, you were.

Wednesday, 9:11 p.m.

Oh, my precious. I'm really having a rough time. I see you in everything, and yet, you're not there. One minute, I'm so proud of everything you were, the next minute, I'm weeping over losing you. It just doesn't get any better. My feelings, my pain, are almost as raw as when you died; at times, I don't want to go on without you. What point is there to life without you? What is life without you? But I know people and family are counting on me. So…I can't give up. I must not give up.

Back to the Lord is my Shepherd. The short time in prayer was wonderful. I have resolved to be there much earlier for prayer. Since so much of my prayer time is spent weeping. Maybe in my brokenness, God can use me. So much hatred and division in the world. So much screaming and accusing each other. All the things that made someone with your love and integrity wince and pray.

I am modeling my life after yours. To be quieter and more loving and patient. To try and be more like our Savior. Goodnight, my darling. Pray for me, please.

Thursday, August 8th, 7:48 am.

Good morning, my beautiful wife. You never accepted that you were beautiful and special. None of us could ever convince you that it was true. Now you know, I hope, I'm coming to the conclusion of something I already know—that my only hope of battling this constant grief and pain is helping others. I will continue to do that. But I can start thinking of you anytime, anywhere, and begin to weep. I'm a mess. Only God can fix me, that's for sure. To finish what God called us to do will take a few years. Then I can be with you. I want to spend time with children and grandchildren. Maybe from me, they can learn about you. About the most amazing woman who ever lived.

QUIET PEOPLE LEAVE LEGACIES THAT OUTLIVE THEM

Proverbs 13:22 – "A good man leaves an inheritance to his children's children…"

Proverbs 11:12 (ESV) – "Whoever belittles his neighbor lacks sense, but a man of understanding remains silent."

Romans 12:2 – "And do not be conformed to this world, but be transformed by the renewing of your mind, that you may prove what is that good and acceptable and perfect will of God."

James 1:19-20 – "¹⁹ Know this, my beloved brothers: let every person be quick to hear, slow to speak, slow to

*anger; ²⁰ for the anger of man does not
produce the righteousness of God."*

WHEN I USE THE PHRASE "QUIET
people," I'm not just talking about people who don't
speak loudly; I'm talking about those who are not
always out in front of everything and every event—the
people who work behind the scenes to make sure everything works. They go about their day letting others who
are so often at the center of attention get the credit for
something that many people had a hand in doing.

In the church world, the speakers, the musicians,
and the singers seem to get all the attention. It can seem
that they are the most important people in the kingdom
of God. This might be entirely how man looks at things,
but I can assure you that God does not look at us this
way. He sees the little mothers in the church who are
faithful in all they do, who pray constantly for not only
their families but the church and the nation. These are
the ones God will honor in heaven. In this life, He
is ever mindful of what is really happening. And as
someone has said, life is a training ground for eternity.

It's interesting that Jesus compared His followers to
salt and light. He explained that both of those elements
change the environment around them, and He tells us
that we should do just that. Salt and light produce no

sound, but they cause change. Quiet people do the same. They live out the adage that says, "Actions speak louder than words." They know that if they just calm down and remain quiet, their circumstances will improve. Terry was such a person. In fact, she found enjoyment in doing things quietly.

The Bible also speaks of angels unawares. I'm not saying that Terry was an actual angel—I mean, she was my angel—but in a way, quiet people who leave a legacy with their lives are like angels we don't recognize. Even in the secular world, the loudest, most profane people often get all the attention. The stars with the most outrageous, perverted lifestyles dominate the news, and the richest people, no matter if they made their riches honestly or not, get all the admiration.

This is especially true of politicians and news pundits, who seem to make the most noise, screaming and shouting outlandish, mean, worthless, and even, at times, untrue statements. The noise can be deafening, but if you want peace of mind, just don't listen to it. Occasionally, allow yourself to turn it off, and give your mind and your spirit rest. Besides, my father used to say, "It's the empty wagon that makes the most noise." Don't be impressed with all the show and go, with all the noise and posturing. Believe me, when the chips are down, it's all show and no go, and more is always said than done.

Give me quiet people any day over every loud person who ever lived. The greatest wisdom of quiet people is their choice to think before they speak. They understand that you rarely get in trouble for speaking too little. Quiet people, like teachers, first responders, nurses, caregivers, housewives, soldiers, bus drivers, clerks, and missionaries all go about their daily business, doing a good job without ever expecting someone to be standing by, watching, clapping, or constantly giving them accolades.

Proverbs 17:27-28 – "Even a fool is counted wise when he holds his peace; When he shuts his lips, he is considered perceptive."

As Mark Twain said, "It is better to remain silent and be thought a fool than to open one's mouth and remove all doubt."

Ecclesiastes 3:7 – "there is a time to be silent and a time to speak."

Proverbs 10:19 – "In the multitude of words sin is not lacking, but he who restrains his lips is wise."

Proverbs 21:23 – "Whoever guards his mouth and tongue keeps his soul from troubles."

Terry was a quiet and thoughtful person, so we shared lots of silent time together. Often, we would just be reading, but there were times when we would watch TV with each other. Interestingly, though, I haven't felt like I wanted to watch TV since Terry died, or even use much social media, for that matter. I know I'll watch it again sometime, but for now, I'm enjoying the peace and quiet. It's funny—I haven't missed the news, sports, drama, or anything. I have my phone, which allows me to keep up with news I choose to watch, although only occasionally.

Cutting back on TV and social media has allowed me more time to meditate on spiritual matters and reflect on Terry's wonderful life. This has helped me in my journey of healing. I haven't isolated myself, but I have restricted what's coming into my mind, which helps me to feel refreshed without all the screaming and noise.

From now on, I think I will occasionally back away from the noise of what sounds almost like being in a room with dozens of two-year-old children squabbling over toys. I keep hoping that maybe in time, some of them will grow up, become adults, and settle down. In the meantime, I'm comfortable with God and His Word as my companions. Terry was so good at turning down the noise around us. She loved *Psalm 46:10: "Be still and know that I am God."*

Today, it's obvious that we as a country and society do everything to the extreme. We overindulge in everything, letting too much from outside sources into our minds and our lives. Yet you can be well informed without being over informed. I guess we have lost the discipline to restrict certain things in our lives, which has not made us stronger, but weaker. Many times, quiet people are thinking people, and they already know that, in so many areas of our lives, less is always more.

Also, quiet people, like Terry, rarely show anger. She beautifully represented the following verse:

> *Ephesians 4:26-27 (ESV) – "Be angry and do not sin; do not let the sun go down on your anger, [27] and give no opportunity to the devil."*

When something really displeased her, Terry would frown and get very quiet while she thought everything through. Then, when she spoke, she never attacked; instead, she would graciously, respectfully, and quietly explain why she disagreed. If you are young, I know you are probably thinking, *Those are old-fashioned manners and have no place in the world we live in today.* That's where I would respectfully disagree with you.

Yes, it is true that good manners have been around for a long time, but in my mind, they are timeless. If you want to be strong and have control over a situation, have good manners. You see, when you are dealing with people and situations, manners make everything easier. They are also a cushion that helps us keep from insulting and hurting one another.

Over the course of her life, Terry had impeccable manners, at all times and in every situation, no matter how tense. She would systematically love, respect, forgive, and then pray for someone, which enabled her to bring change into many lives. Even though she was quiet, her actions were not meek or weak, but rather strong, bold, and effective.

> "Rudeness is the weak person's imitation of strength." – Eric Hoffer

> "Good manners and kindness are always in fashion." – Anonymous

"There are some things that money can't buy, like good manners, morals, and integrity." – Anonymous

"Good manners are just a way of showing other people that we have respect for them." – Bill Kelly

"He that cannot forgive others breaks the bridge over which he himself must pass of he would ever reach heaven; for everyone has need to be forgiven." – George Herbert

Terry practiced forgiving. She loved this scripture:

Colossians 3:12-13 – "Therefore, as the elect of God, holy and beloved, put on tender mercies, kindness, humility, meekness, longsuffering; [13] bearing with one another, and forgiving one another, if anyone has a complaint against another; even as Christ forgave you, so you also must do."

She would so often caution and admonish me to forgive, no matter the situation or the person who had upset me. She would say, "Simply the best and only answer to this situation is to pray and forgive that person." After I had huffed and puffed a while, I soon and always realized that she was right, and I would pray and ask God to forgive me for not forgiving others.

Psalms 46:10 – "Be still, and know that I am God."

Lamentations 3:26 – "It is good that one should hope and wait quietly for the salvation of the Lord."

Isaiah 26:3 – "You will keep him in perfect peace, whose mind is stayed on You, because he trusts in You."

1 Timothy 6:6-7 – "Now godliness with contentment is great gain. [7] For we brought nothing into this world, and it is certain we can carry nothing out."

Also, many quiet people are unselfish, like Terry, who always wanted other people to receive things rather than her. Terry loved to give. She willingly gave her tithes and offerings to our church because she believed in its ministry. Consistently, she put pressure on us as a church to fulfill our commitment to giving to foreign and local missions.

Before Terry died, she made sure that whatever of our little estate would be left after we passed away, a large part of hers would go to missions—where her heart was—to people who are hurting, to people in need. She would say, "We have enough. Let's share."

If you are reading this, I know you must be thinking that I am embellishing Terry's life because I loved her so much, but I'm not. If anything, I'm not saying enough about her. She was so much more than all of this.

And that is my point about quiet people. We overlook and underestimate them, for our attention is frequently drawn away by the glitter and noise that keep us from seeing the quiet treasure that is so often right beside us. Many times, we are the ones making all that noise, and we miss the chance to hear something important from a quiet person. Maybe it's time for us to quit talking, be quiet, and learn from others who are not trying to be the center of attention.

14

I HOPE THERE IS SOMEONE WHO WILL PICK UP HER MANTLE

Proverbs 19:17 – "He who has pity on the poor lends to the Lord, and He will pay back what he has given."

Matthew 16:24-25 – "Then Jesus said to His disciples, 'If anyone desires to come after Me, let him deny himself, and take up his cross, and follow Me.[25]*For whoever desires to save his life will lose it, but whoever loses his life for My sake will find it.'"*

AS I HAVE SAID BEFORE, I WAS COMpletely devastated when my precious wife, Terry, died on May 25, 2019. I couldn't imagine how I would go on without her. It took me only a day to realize that there was a huge hole in my life—an emptiness that only she could fill, for she had filled it every day we were together. Not only did she do this for me, but also for our church and everyone she met. Shortly after her death, one of her god-daughters told me that she didn't know if she wanted to live in a world without Terry Shaffer Hall. I completely agreed because she made everything and everyone around her better.

Her mission in life, her ministry, and her Mantle was to model her life after the love of Christ. When she died, she left that Mantle for other people to pick up and carry on. That is her legacy. I, for one, volunteer to pick up part of that Mantel, but at my age, I need some younger people to pick it up with me.

How do we pick up that Mantle? How do we carry on what Terry so faithfully ministered every day? By looking at her life and realizing that she modeled it after Christ's teachings. When it is time to pick up someone's Mantle, that usually means that person's life has come to an end, which is the case here. Often, God places someone special in our lives as a beacon of light to point us to His Word. He uses this person to nudge us to act and to live according to the precepts of the Bible, to not wait for some loud, seemingly important people to declare themselves leaders. God has placed these quiet lights in our life as examples to follow.

I know I have my work cut out for me on this journey, and I know it will only be possible with God's comfort, help, and direction, as well as Terry's help and direction. Thankfully, I have her life to look to as an example. One of her scriptures that I stand on every day is this:

Proverbs 3:5-6 – "Trust in the Lord with all your heart, and lean not on your own understanding; [6] in all your ways acknowledge Him, and He shall direct your paths."

Part of Terry's legacy was her ability to watch what she said in response to everything. She knew that words had power, so she was always careful with her words. In her wisdom, she was aware that words can hurt or help, tear down or build up, bring conflict or bring peace, bring division or bring unity, spread fuel on a fire or spread water to put out the fire. That is one legacy of her Mantle that we would be wise to pick up.

Proverbs 17:27-28 – "He who has knowledge spares his words, and a man of understanding is of a calm spirit. [28] Even a fool is counted wise when he

holds his peace; when he shuts his lips,
he is considered perceptive."

Ephesians 4:29 – "Let no corrupt word
(or foul word) proceed out of your
mouth, but what is good for necessary
edification, that it may impart grace to
the hearers."

Terry's love for reading the Bible began as soon as she became a Christian. She always had a hunger for knowledge, and once she was born again, she read the Bible and meditated on it every day.

Her wisdom was enhanced and expanded when she became a student of the Bible. As she quietly read God's Word, she would just shake her head in agreement from time to time. She would say, "This is our GPS; this is our how-to manual. All the answers to life are in this book if we just read it." That's why she inspired people to read it. She spent twenty-six years as co-director of the US Capitol Bible Reading Marathon, encouraging and helping people read through this sacred book. She called it the "book of books," knowing it is historical and has had a spiritual impact on much of the world.

Terry knew and appreciated the Bible's impact on different aspect of society, such as speech, culture, and music. She also knew the freedoms our nation enjoyed came from the Bible and that if we really read and obeyed God's Word, our nation would be better, because it would change us. Often, she would say, "Just read it."

I watched as Terry encouraged legislators, administrative aides, policemen, housewives, home-schooled children, Christian schools, pastors, lay people, homeless people, and various citizens of this wonderful country, as well as citizens from around the world, all to read God's Holy Word, the Bible. I wonder who will have a passion like her to read the Bible?

The Bible meant everything to Terry. It was her companion, her adviser, her sustainer in dark times, her encourager when she was down, her final truth on so many issues. She read it, studied it, meditated on it, quoted it, and lived by it every day. She loved it. Yes, she questioned why she was dying, why we couldn't live out our dreams and plans, but she also took comfort in the scriptures she knew so well. Although she questioned, she was not afraid. She was sad that she was dying but accepted it as God's will, not ours. I can't tell you the tears we shed working through that.

Although the Bible was the most significant book in Terry's life, her love for literature was truly inspiring. At one time, our library contained hundreds of her books on literature. Up until right before she died, she continued to love reading literature. But when she found the book of books, her special book, the Bible, God's love letter from home to her, she felt it put everything in life into perspective. Still, she didn't pretend to understand everything, for she knew that many of the things she was reading were mysteries that she would have to wait to understand. Now, she completely understands, because she is with the living Word, her Savior, Jesus Christ.

She loved to meditate on God and spend time in prayer. I think her prayers were what kept our marriage so wonderfully low key, loving, and exciting, and I also believe they gave strength to our ministry.

Terry drew so much knowledge and strength from her time in prayer, and she felt that prayer and reading the Bible were the two bulwarks of her Christian faith. It worried her that so many Christians today were drifting away from these two essential, foundational parts of our faith. She would tell everyone, "These are the basics. We must get back to them on a daily basis. We must understand that one of the attributes of God is righteousness. And part of that for us is daily doing what is right." And living rightly is what she did.

Of course, the biggest part of Terry's Mantle was loving people. Some thirty years ago, a family from Ethiopia appeared at our church door, homeless, seeking asylum in this country. Immediately, Terry surrounded them with love and began working to find help for them from every source. I remember her asking a religious friend and neighbor who worked for the state department for help, but this friend refused and chewed Terry out for helping them. Terry just smiled and said, "I'm sorry, I have to help them. I'm compelled to. I'm a Christian. Don't worry, I'll find help." And she did; amazingly, she remained friends with our neighbor. Today, the thirty-plus family members from Ethiopia, well, they are part of our family and continue to pay us back in love—they even became citizens and great assets to this country.

Even during the last few years and months of her life, Terry was busy loving and helping immigrants from South America, most of whom were documented, but some might have been undocumented—we never knew. She loved them all so much that she would have given her life for them. Her huge reservoir of love allowed her to make a difference in anyone.

Someone once asked me why I never seem to be impressed with so many famous and powerful people. I'm not. How can I be? When I compare them to my amazing wife, they don't stand a chance.

TIME IS STILL NOT ENOUGH

IN THIS NEW SEASON OF MY LIFE, everywhere I go, I see couples constantly fussing and fighting, ignoring, insulting, and belittling each other. Whether it's in a store, in a restaurant, or in the car, they seem to never stop bickering. Sometimes, I watch individuals treat their mate with less respect than they would a stranger, and some just take them for granted. I want to say to all of them, "Just stop! Please! Someday, I promise you, you will regret every one of those actions and words. You are only going to have one life together here. Be conscious of how important each minute you have together is."

If you really love each other, I think you will someday regret what you are doing. Dedicate your life to cherishing and loving your husband or wife. Always respect them. Always work toward building them up, rather than tearing them down. Always be quick to apologize and forgive, and be happy and proud when they succeed. These actions help to nurture the most wonderful relationship. I can tell you that because that is what Terry and I did, and it made every minute of our almost forty-nine years together wonderful. They were so full of life, fulfilled expectations, love, and now, memories that I cherish.

Over the years, we took on so many projects together. When I look back and remember how little money we had and I think about the things Terry was able to accomplish by scrounging around and getting the best prices or second-hand items, I am amazed.

She was able to do anything with what she had. Her hands were all the remodeling our old church on Capitol Hill, refurbishing it into a beautiful, bright house of worship. She built relationships with several historic departments in DC, who willingly helped us get the proper historical supplies. Even with these great accomplishments, she also swept, cleaned, painted. She was always happy to be doing anything for the glory of God.

I can still see her standing by those beautiful white walls with her arms lifted, praising God, tears running down her cheeks. Even now, in our church in Camp Springs, Maryland, I sometimes think I see her in the back of the church, and I want to run and take her in my arms.

No, time isn't enough. Without her presence, there is a gigantic hole in our ministry and our church. And here I am, a few months after my wife's death, still feeling that emptiness.

As I explained in the first part of this book, in September of 2018, I promised Terry I would begin taking her to Martha's Vineyard for ten days each month. I asked permission of the church, and they so lovingly said yes. At that moment, I had no idea that we were just nine months away from her death.

From September to April, we went once a month. We would spend hours sitting and looking at the ocean, talking about how wonderful it was and how wonderful our future would be there.

Terry was so happy each time we went—happier than in any place we had ever been. She was a different person there. I cherish every day we had together on that island. Was I worried about our future? Yes, but I was still hoping and praying for a miraculous remission so that we could have at least five more years together in our little corner of paradise.

The last two times we went up, I began to worry more. I had to make the back seat of our SUV into a special place for her to travel. Because her medicine prevented her from being in direct sunlight, I blacked out the window. I also put blankets on the floor because the neuropathy in her feet caused such pain, and I filled the car with pillows, blankets, a small ice chest for cold drinks, and a plug for her iPhone. I tried to make the car a comfortable little compartment for traveling. Terry would put her feet on the armrest and on my right arm so I could feel her there. I wish I could feel that again.

I treasure those seven or eight months. We cooked delicious meals, ate good food, and had neighbors and friends over. Every time we were there, we would go to Terry's favorite place for breakfast once, so she could have her beloved blueberry pancakes. We held each other in our arms and looked at our beautiful, peaceful view of the ocean. While there, I had no idea it would be my last trip with her.

During our time on the island, we talked about the Lord and our hopes for our future. Even though we were afraid to say it, I think we were beginning to see our future slipping away. We just held each other and cried.

On one trip, I came down with a nasty case of pneumonia. Bless her heart, Terry took me to the hospital for an overnight stay, then we both just laid on the sofas and commiserated with our ailments.

Only later did a dear friend share that Terry had told her she thought that trip was her last one up there. Terry had spoken with several people about not thinking she was going to beat this battle with cancer. I wish I had known, so I could have encouraged her more. Just thinking about it now, it brings me to tears.

In the Bible, Jeremiah was known as the weeping prophet. It looks like I will be known as the weeping pastor. People have asked me how long will I continue to grieve for my wife. Probably as long as I live. But won't that grief immobilize me and isolate me? No, I realize that God has allowed this grief into my life, and far from destroying me, it is remaking me. Through this grief, God is working on me. Through this grief, I am becoming closer to Him. Through this grief, He is going to use me for His glory. My dear friend and co-worker, Pastor Stratton, quoted this to me: "Grieving is a process that God uses to bring us to a place of wholeness. Grieving is His great gift to us. It is a necessary part of our journey. Healing." This speaks comfort to my soul.

And if, like me, you are suffering from grief, this is what I tell myself every morning: "Get up. Get going. Get out. Get something done today!" So far, it's been working for me.

At this point, I realize that I am a widowed man, diminished by the loss of an amazing wife, but I'm still in the battle. My strength is returning, and I am determined to give my remaining life to others.

I encourage you to recognize the incredible gift of friends that God has given you. Two of my closest friends, Mark and Lora Batterson, came so often to pray and lift Terry's spirits when she was suffering. Terry and I would just sit in the presence of the Lord and let them minister to us. I use them as an example to show you that God has someone near you who is waiting to encourage you.

My grief, however, is still with me, for even though we had a long life together, our time wasn't nearly enough because our life was so wonderful. When our life together came to a close, I had to decide whether or not I had the will to go on. Now I know that I do.

What we had lasted through time and will last through eternity. Even though I am going on alone without her, I certainly don't want anyone to replace her. Our marriage was perfect and complete, for time and eternity. With her death, the chapter of marriage was finished without any other chapters to be added. Her memories are enough to sustain me from now till I see again. So, in her honor, I am determined to continue on with our ministry.

Some have asked if I question God about Terry dying. Yes, of course I do. Do I feel that it is unfair? Absolutely! I also ask Him, "Why? Why? Why?" I ask myself if I could have done more. Yes, I could have done more. But I did what I could to the best of my ability at the time. Don't beat yourself up over things like this. I can assure you that questioning God in no way diminishes His love for me or you, for one of His most important attributes is love.

God's Word says that His thoughts and His ways are beyond ours. I have to accept that, knowing that I will one day understand. I console myself by believing that Terry's work here was done, so God called her home, just like when my work here is done, He will call me home as well.

Until then, I plan to pick up Terry's Mantle and do what I can to the best of my ability with the time I have. I hope I live long enough to make a difference like she did. I love young people, so I will turn to them for help. I love being around them and hearing and supporting their plans and dreams for their future. Maybe some of them will pick up her Mantle with me.

The only moment when time will become enough is when I face my own death. I am not afraid of dying, especially now. When I die, I will be happy to have finished the work God has called me to do, and I will be delighted to see my wife again. I have decided to live, so God can use me any place I am needed, and when He is finished with me, I want Him to take me home to see my precious Terry, who I miss every minute of every day I am without her.

To my darling wife, I know you never wanted me or anyone to talk about you, to praise you for how beautiful and wonderful you were or how you amazed us when you did such important things so quietly. Well, get used to it. I can't stop talking about you. My love, you know I've barely scratched the surface of your life.

So, dear one, if you have made it this far with me, let me say that I had no intention of trying to answer all the questions about grief, just a few about my own. I hope in some way this little book has helped you, and I pray that Terry's life will continue to help you on your own journey.

Let me close by saying, treasure every minute and every day you are blessed to have with the one you love. Remember everything you did to fall in love, and keep doing those things, even if you have been together a long time. Keep the flame of love alive. Even in the last six months of Terry's life, people in our church would comment on how we couldn't keep our eyes off of each other. This was because we had made sure to keep the love we first had alive for all those years.

Don't be selfish and do just what you want to do; always find a way to include your loved one in your plans. Get rid of the "I" in your relationship and focus more the "we." In the years to come, you will treasure those memories—I promise you. No matter how long you have, you will never feel that it is enough. If, however, you have made the right preparations with God, eternity will be enough.

As an old pastor, I encourage you to treasure your walk with God. If you are grieving, let Him sustain you. Let His Word, the Holy Bible, be your comfort, inspiration, and guide and give you purpose.

I hope something about Terry's life and ministry of love to everyone inspires you. This beautiful, fascinating, thoroughly converted woman inspired me each day we had together. Right now, I feel that this is a good place to stop. Since I have been talking about her Mantle, I probably need to pick it up and get to work. With that Mantle, I'm going to find new joy and new strength to finish her legacy. I don't know how Elisha felt when he picked up Elijah's Mantle, but I'm pretty excited about what lies ahead of me.

May God go with you each step of your journey.

My darling Terry, with my last breath
I will whisper your name.

ACKNOWLEDGEMENTS

DEAR ONE, THANK YOU FOR READING these few words about the woman I loved. You may be young, or you may be old. If you are hurting, you need comfort, and I pray that you may find comfort in your time of grief as I have. Yes, I admit, I still cry every day over my loss. I probably always will. But in time, I know the wounds will heal, even though I will always have scars. In time, I will be able to smile and laugh about all of our good moments together. In time, the joy of our long wonderful relationship will outweigh the pain of my loss.

If you are a close friend or relative who loved Terry, there is only one way to see her again—through surrendering your life to Christ.

May the peace of God be with you. May He keep, comfort, and console you, giving you the peace only He can give. That is my prayer for you.

Lastly, I would like to thank several people for helping me through this time of grief and pain. You were all there for me.

Thank you, Irene, for giving birth to the most amazing daughter. You poured all you love into her, and because of that, she poured her love into people, changing many lives.

Thank you to my sister Judy and her husband Ralph who check on me daily to make sure I'm ok. My sister Troyce and her husband Jerry, Troyce, you were my sounding board for this book. My brother Tony and his wife Brenda, thank you for texting me often. My nephew Justin and his wife Cynthia., I know you are there for me whenever I need you. All of you comforted me and lifted my spirits when my heart was completely broken.

Thank you, Jeremy Caleb and Gabrielle, for coming to take care of your old uncle. Thank you to our precious daughter Sheri and her husband Ron for being with Terry before she died and holding her and me in your heart. Thank you, dear daughter-in-law Phylis, for your prayers and words of love and comfort. Thank you, Trent and Krista, for your love and concern. Thank you, Tristan and Kyle, for your prayers and love as well. Thank you, Brett and Sheri, for your love and coming to see her, and Brett, for your phone calls. Thank you,

Jeremy and Mitzi, for your love, your prayers, and your words of comfort.

Thank you, our precious daughters, Michelle, Saba, and Rahel. You were with her the last day she was here. What a comfort that was to her.

Thank you, my precious church family. Each of you mean more to me than you will ever know. To my dear Pastor Stratton and Pastor Smallwood, you lovingly held my hand each step during my grief. To my elders, my ministers, thank you for your love, your prayers, and your wise words of comfort.

Thank you, Pastor Alveraz, Rosa, and your family for all the love and help you provided us during our two-year battle. And you're still standing with me.

Thank you, Mark and Lora, for your friendship. Thank you for your love and support. From that strength, I've dared to share my grief, with the hope that it will in some way help others.

Thank you, MV family—Judy, Jason, Joan, Addie, Leah, David, and Sal. You and MV were an important part of Terry's dream, in her little place in paradise.

And thank you, Terry, for our wonderful life and love together. Thank you for loving me. I'll never be finished talking about you, my love. You are so much more than these few words can ever describe. You will live forever in my dreams, my thoughts, and my memories. Till we meet again and pick up where we left off and you take me in your arms, smile that smile, and kiss me. Till then, my darling, I will never stop loving you. May our Lord and Savior Jesus Christ get all the glory and praise from this book.

Jill Wyman, dear friend, thank you for helping me put my book together.

CPSIA information can be obtained
at www.ICGtesting.com
Printed in the USA
BVHW020835120320
574664BV00013B/5

9 781630 507596